Mexican Food

How to Prepare Traditional Mexican Food at Home with Over 100 Recipes Cookbook

By

Adele Tyler

Table Of Content

Introduction

Mexican food is considered as one of the most famous cuisines in the world. Whether we talk about enchiladas, tacos, or tortillas, it is loved by people from different countries in the world. Mexican delights have satisfied the taste buds of many food-lovers. Popular Mexican recipes are available in many restaurants worldwide, as Mexican dishes are much more than just spicy salsa and guacamole. They have the culinary influence of many cultures that have led to today's Mexican colorful and vibrant cuisine. Traditional Mexican food has a wide variety of colorful and healthy ingredients used in it. Mexican recipes are prepared with fresh produce, fiber-packed tortillas, protein-filled beans, and nutritious spices like garlic, chilies, cloves, cumin, and cinnamon.

The best way to celebrate Mexican food's rich history is to try and make these delicious and tasty recipes at home. They are super easy to make. This cookbook has over 100 Mexican recipes for you, from breakfast, lunch, dinner, soups, and desserts, to vegetarian as well as non-vegetarian. This cookbook will help you become pro at making this cuisine at home. There is no other way to have full control over what you eat than to cook at home. You can always customize your recipes, making it healthier without compromising its taste and pure essence.

Knowing about the food history of a particular culture has always been fun. It connects us more to that culture and its cuisines. A small part of this book has been dedicated to the history of Mexican food, the traditional Mexican food ingredients, and the evolution of Mexican food in the United States. In chapter two, the health benefits of Mexican food, and the preference of its homemade cooking has been addressed, which is crucial to maintain a balance in your recipes.

You will find different varieties of Mexican breakfast recipes in this cookbook, from Mexican Baked Eggs, Breakfast Tostada, and Sunrise Sausage Enchiladas to Breakfast Tacos and Eggs & Chorizo Wraps.

In this cookbook, there is a long list of delicious Mexican lunch and dinner recipes. From trying Prawn & Chorizo Quesadilla, Grilled Cumin Lime Chicken, and Mexican Lasagna to Chicken Fajitas and Refried Beans, you will never be short of the choices. For a healthy eating lifestyle, the addition of soup in your daily meal plan can do a lot of good. Find a variety of Mexican soups recipes in this cookbook that are super easy to make at home. A separate portion has been reserved for healthy Mexican vegetarian recipes for veggie-lovers to make the most out of the fresh vegetables.

No menu is complete without salads and desserts. Make the best out of this cookbook, and try some mouth-watering salad and dessert dishes. You will also find the most famous Mexican tacos, burritos, and quesadillas recipes in this cookbook. Each dish is filled with tasty, healthy, and colorful ingredients. Whether you are cooking just for yourself or preparing for a family gathering, this cookbook has a much more satisfying list of incredible recipes to get ready for Mexican Feast.

Chapter 1: History of Mexican Food

Mexican food has a diverse and long history. Some people believe that traditional Mexican food has a significant influence of Mayan Indians, who were gatherers and nomadic hunters. Corn tortillas having bean paste in it was a very common food for them apart from fish, wild and tropical fruits. On the other hand, salsa was derived from the Aztec market. In Spanish, it is used for the sauce. In modern salsa, you can find tomatillo, red tomatoes, chipotle, and avocado. These core ingredients are the same as the past recipe of salsa. In 1885, enchilada was first used in the U.S., but Aztecs had the direct link with the concept and recipe of tortillas as they used it as a wrap.

Aztecs domesticated the tomatillo, which is a fruit. Tomatillo means plump and round. Today, a fruit very similar to tomatillo is very common in the U.S. It provides a tart flavor green sauces. Let's look at the influence of different cultures on Mexican food and Mexican food evolution in the U.S.

1.1 Influence of Different Cultures on Mexican Food

Mexican food has significant influences of different cultures due to the past colonization eras. That increased later on due to the trade between various colonies and countries when globalization started to grow. Mexican food is thus a result of many diverse cultural influences. It has also adopted ingredients and different cooking styles from various cultures.

Mayan Influence

Mayan Indians brought significant culinary influence on Mexican food. They used to live in the Yucatan in Southeast Mexico.

As mentioned earlier, Mayan Indians were gatherers and hunters, so most of their food included many animals like deer, raccoons, armadillos, rabbits, rattlesnakes, spider monkeys, iguanas, pigeons, frogs, turtles, and turkeys. Apart from that, their food also included beans, tropical fruits, and corn. These influences still have been retained in Mexican cooking. This type of food is now well known as Comida prehispánica, or pre-Hispanic cuisine. It is looked at as an exotic cuisine in Mexico's food today.

Aztec Influence

Aztec tribes conquered Mexico and rules over it in the mid-1300s. They added salt, chili peppers, chocolate, and honey into the culinary mix of Mayan Indians. Avocados, tomatoes, and squash became popular. Salt and chili peppers became as crucial for them as they are today in our cuisines. It had a significant influence on their food. Modern Azteca Mexican cuisines still use those traditional Mayan ingredients while adding new flavors as well.

Spanish Influence

Like many countries in the world, Mexico was also under colonization. Spanish invaded colonized Mexico in 1521. They introduced their dishes and recipes to Mexican culture like olive oil, rice, garlic, cinnamon, coriander, and other spices. They brought domesticated animals like sheep, pigs, cows, goats, and chickens. The goats, sheep, and cows were sources of dairy, and cheese became the main ingredient in most of the dishes. They also brought changes to cooking methods.

After the invasion, the Spanish soldiers found out that the cuisine consisted of corn-based recipes with herbs and chilies, tomatoes, and beans.

Then they combined imported addition of rice, pork, beef, chicken garlic, onions, and wine with the local foods of Mexico that mostly included beans, tomatoes, chocolate, corn, avocado, vanilla, papaya, chili peppers, pineapple, squash, peanuts, sweet potato, turkey, and fish.

The Spanish influence led to many dishes such as Chile Rellenos, lomo en adobo, and quesadillas.

French Influence

When the French invaded Mexico, they brought a variety of fantastic baked foods with them. Mexican bolillo and sweetbreads are some examples of French influence. They also introduced various cooking techniques. The combination of their techniques with the Mexican ingredients proved to be fantastic. Mexican ingredients like avocados and squash blossoms were perfect for the French style crepes, mousse, and soups.

1.2 Traditional Mexican Food Ingredients

The three ingredients that have always been in Mexican food before the arrival of Spanish influence are beans, corn, and chilies. Corn was being used in all forms, but mostly consumed as a tortilla. In making quesadillas and tacos today, tortilla is used. Apart from that, tomatoes, avocado, and rice are also used in Mexican dishes today.

Before the arrival of Spaniards, meat was not abundant, so Mexicans used to include beans and corn as the main nutritional ingredients. Heavy spices and chiles were used for a complex flavor in their dishes.

Chile Peppers

The use of chiles is the specialty of Mexican food, and it makes perfect sense as chiles have their deep roots in Mexico. They have always been part of Mexican cuisine.

Even if you go back to thousands of years, the use of chiles was common. Different types of chiles are used in Mexican food like aromatic ancho, spicy jalapeno, and fiery serrano. They are the main ingredients in most of the Mexican food, even the classic cuisines as well. Chiles are not just used as a spice, but they also add a special flavor to recipes. Many recipes almost use some kind of chile. They are used as whole, fresh, smoked, powdered, or dried.

Beans

Another ingredient that is most widely used is frijoles or beans. You hardly find any kitchen in Mexico that is without a wide variety of beans. They have different types. Most known are the black beans, pinto beans, brownish, and the black beans flor de junio and golden Peruvian. Beans are used in dishes like refried beans, soups, bean salads, and the traditional recipe of frijoles de olla.

Corn

Corn is the key source of grain in Mexico. Mostly it is dried. It is widely used in making tamales, beverages, soups, and tortillas. The corn tortilla is included in almost every recipe in Mexico. Apart from that, huitlacoche grown on corn ears is found in various dishes in Mexican food like omelets, succotash, as a filling in tamales or tacos.

Avocado

The Hass avocado is cultivated in Mexico. It is the main and key ingredient in "guac". It is also found in salsas, salads, and tacos topping.

Tomatoes

Vegetables are widely used in Mexican food, especially tomatoes. The raw and fresh tomatoes are the key ingredient found in salsas.

They have also used as fillings toppings for burritos and tacos. They are not commonly employed in making a red sauce in Mexico with red chiles as their main ingredient. The freshly cooked as well as canned tomatoes add flavor to salads, rice, and soups.

Herbs

Mexican oregano and cilantro are the most commonly found herbs in Mexican cuisines. Cilantro is mostly used fresh that brings brightness and also the citrus essence to recipes. The vibrant green color is snipped and adds a sense of esthetics to salsas, guacamole, and other dishes. The Mexican oregano is locally used in Mexico. It can be utilized as dried or fresh.

1.3 Evolution of Popular Mexican Foods in U.S.

Mexican food has influenced many American cuisines for years. In the 20th century, many Mexican-inspired recipes have been there in almost every corner of the U.S., making their way to the mainstream dishes. Apart from the traditional recipes like tacos, tortillas, tamales, salsas, enchiladas, many new recipes emerged in the U.S. that was a perfect blend of regional American, Mexican, and Latino culture.

Enchiladas

Enchiladas are mostly topped with onion rings, fresh cheese, and fresh cream in Mexico. But in the U.S., enchilada is usually topped with the melted cheese, and then served with pico de gallo, Mexican rice, refried beans, shredded lettuce, and guacamole. Enchilada is a straightforward dish, though it does not look like that, nut it surely is.

Tacos

In Mexico, you can enjoy tacos with pork, beef, or chicken. Tacos have their roots back to mid-19th century.

Mexico was developing in its industrialization during this period. Early tacos were used to be filled with organ meats (inexpensive) and some other ingredients. Tacos were brought to the U.S. in the early 1900s. They had the same appearance as we see them in Mexican-American style taco today; the U-shaped tortilla shells filled with iceberg lettuce, ground beef, and the cheddar cheese.

Salsa

Salsa is a sauce in Mexican recipes. Some people think salsa is a spicy tomato-based red sauce. But, in Mexico, it is a term used for the sauce. Salsa has a long history back to the era of Aztecs in Mexico. It is found in different forms like salsa verde, which is made of tomatillos, cilantro, jalapenos, pico de gallo, that uses chopped tomatoes, garlic, and seasoned with lime juice and oil. Pace Foods introduced to salsa in the U.S. in 1947. Today, you can easily find salsa at any grocery store to enjoy it with the tortilla chips.

Tex-Mex

Refried Beans

The taste of Mexican food and the popularity of Mexican Cuisine led to the several variations in its recipes across many countries and regions. Tex-Mex dish evolved in Southwest America in Texas-Mexico. It is a variation of the traditional recipe with an American touch. The best example of Tex-Mex recipes is refried beans. Tex-Mex is, however, different from the original Mexican recipe. It includes, to a certain extent, some of the same ingredients, but it is not exactly like that.

New Mexican Cuisine

New Mexican Cuisine is a kind of the regional cuisine that originates from New Mexico in the U.S., and also in southern Colorado. It is known as a subset of the Mexican-American cuisine. The American consumers' liking Mexican food has certainly evolved since a long time.

Mexican food is a perfect blend of all the cultures mentioned above. However, you can still find diversity in the recipes as per the Mexican regional differences. Mexican food has variations according to the region, local climate, ethnic differences, and geography. Northern Mexico is best known for beef and meat recipes. Southeastern Mexico is famous for spicy vegetables and chicken-based recipes. Seafood is also commonly used in Mexican states that border the Gulf of Mexico or the Pacific Ocean.

Chapter 2: Health Benefits of Homemade Mexican Food

There are some valid reasons to dine in restaurants, including saving time and convenience. There is also another reason not to cook at home: there are a lot of people who think they cannot cook or lack proper cooking skills. So, they consider it more expensive and time-consuming. But if we can spend most of our day time on our phones and the internet, then why not spend time on cooking, which is a meditation in itself. This attitude has led to many diseases like diabetes and obesity in many countries. Restaurant food has some unhealthy portions of our diet, which we can control at home.

Let's look at some general benefits of cooking and eating at home:

- When we dine at a restaurant, there is no way we can find out what goes into our dishes. While cooking at home, they are unlimited healthy options. We can limit the use of certain ingredients to shape it in healthy cuisine.
- Restaurants have a fixed menu to choose from, while at home, we have plenty of options to select and follow some healthy diet plans. We can make whatever we want.
- Developing a healthy eating habit to adopt a healthy lifestyle, and doing that on our terms is only possible at home, not at restaurants. Homemade food offers us a great amount of flexibility.
- Cooking at home bring the family together and strengthens the bond by spending more time together and try new things in the kitchen.
- Cost is cut by a considerable fraction when we choose to cook at home. We have a lot of freedom at all stages of cooking to make it budget-friendly.

Health Benefits of Mexican Food

Mexican food incorporates different pungent flavors in its cuisines. From vegetables to beans, there is a wide variety to choose the ingredients and make healthy Mexican food options without compromising the taste.

Let's look at some fantastic presence of nutrition that we can find in Mexican food:

Fiber

A variety of beans is used in Mexican food. All of these varieties include fiber as a healthy source, a balanced diet. Many people do not take enough fiber that can cause many digestive problems. Tacos or burritos that are made with beans prove to be the healthiest choice. Whole beans have more fiber than refried beans, which are a little bit less nutritious.

Protein

In Mexican food, we can find meat like pork, beef, shrimp, or chicken. When we include lean meat in our diet, it helps in increasing the protein intake. Protein improves the health of muscles and boosts energy levels. Fried meat is delicious, but it adds saturated fats that are not healthy.

Capsaicin

It helps in marinating cholesterol and blood pressure levels, and improve circulation. We can find this in jalapenos, which is used in making Mexican sauces.

Minerals and Vitamins

A variety of vegetables are used in Mexican dishes. These vegetables are the source of some essential nutrients. Onions and tomatoes, for example, are rich in vitamin C.

on the other hand, avocado, which is the key ingredient in making guacamole, provides some healthy unsaturated fats, fiber, and potassium.

Restaurant vs. Homemade Mexican Food

When we think about Mexican food at restaurants, many think of heavy cheeses, fried tortillas, and sour cream in recipes. But, the fact is that traditional Mexican food is much not about that. It is the effect of different cultures that have made the Mexican food what it is today.

Let's see what differentiates homemade Mexican dishes from restaurant dining:

- American restaurants have introduced the heavy use of ingredients like cheese and sour cream. However, at home, there are many endless alternatives to creating a healthy and delicious Mexican recipe. It is not about avoiding those ingredients altogether, it is about limiting the amount that makes it unhealthy.
- Many American households use Mexican food ingredients a lot. People following a healthy eating lifestyle know that keeping balance is the only key to stay healthy. Choose beans and right meats, avoid too much use of cheeses. We can do that at home.
- Authentic and traditional Mexican food always has fresh ingredients in it. Many restaurant chains use the slogan of fresh Mexican food, but never know what is being used back in the kitchen because fresh and healthy go hand-in-hand. We can enjoy both only at home. If eating a healthy bowl is the choice, go for brown rice, lean meat, and beans. Toppings of fresh lettuce and homemade salsa make it even more robust.
- Tacos are a healthy Mexican food option. But if we cook at home, we can choose what we put in a taco shell, and control their portions.

- Use of lean steak, grilled chick, and grilled fish in tacos make an excellent protein-filled diet. There are many healthy options for topping too. Avoid sour cream if you want to make it healthier. We can choose to control these things at home.
- Choosing to make Mexican food healthy is much easier than we think. We can always use the right substitutes. Doing so will not compromise on its essence but makes it even tastier. Add the healthy flavors avocados, onions, and peppers as Mexican ingredients to make the best out of a day's meals.

Chapter 3: Mexican Breakfast Recipes

Cook and enjoy some delicious and healthy Mexican breakfast recipes given in this chapter.

3.1 Eggs and Chorizo Wraps

Ingredients

- 12 ounces chorizo
- 2 tbsp. milk
- 6 eggs, large
- 1 cup cheddar cheese, shredded
- 6 tortillas (6 inches)
- Green onions, thinly sliced
- Fresh cilantro
- Salsa (optional)

Instructions

1. Take a large skillet and cook the chorizo. Keep the heat medium until it is cooked. Drain and put it back to the pan.
2. Take a bowl, and whisk milk and eggs until blended.
3. Pour egg mixture into chorizo. Stir continuously until eggs are thoroughly cooked.
4. Pour cheese in it.
5. Place 1/2 cup mixture in each tortilla.
6. Then add onion, cilantro, and salsa. Fold the tortilla and roll-up.
7. Serve and Enjoy!

3.2 Breakfast Tacos

Ingredients

- 1/2 cup black beans
- 1/2 cup pico de gallo
- 1/2 cup avocado, cubed
- 1 tbsp. lime juice
- 1/2 pound pork sausage
- 1 cup O'Brien potatoes, frozen
- 7 large eggs
- 1/2 cup Monterey Jack shredded cheese
- 2 tbsp. milk
- 6 flour tortillas (8 inches), warmed
- Fresh cilantro, optional
- Sour cream

Instructions

1. Mix avocado, black beans, lime juice, and pico de gallo. Set the mixture aside.
2. Take a large skillet, and cook crumble sausage and potatoes. Keep the heat medium for 5-6 minutes until potatoes are cooked.
3. Mix eggs and milk together. Cook the mixture, and stir continuously and keep the heat medium until eggs are cooked.
4. Pour in the cheese.
5. Put egg mixture into each tortilla.
6. Put a mixture of black bean over top of it.
7. Garnish with cilantro and sour cream.
8. Serve and Enjoy!

3.3 Sunrise Sausage Enchiladas

Ingredients

- 1 pound pork sausage
- 20 ounces hash brown shredded potatoes
- 2 tbsp. canola oil
- 1/2 tsp. salt
- 1/4 tsp. cayenne pepper
- 1/2 tsp. chili powder
- 1/4 tsp. pepper
- 2 cups cheddar cheese, shredded
- 1 can green chiles, chopped
- 8 flour tortillas (8 inches)
- 2 cans enchilada sauce

For Topping:

- Red onion, chopped
- Red pepper, sweet and chopped
- Fresh cilantro, chopped

Instructions

1. Take a skillet and cook sausage on medium heat. Make sure it is not pink anymore. Remove drippings from it while taking it out of the skillet.
2. Heat oil in a pan over medium heat. Cook potatoes until its color is brown. Then turn off the heat.
3. Mix in chiles, seasonings, sausage, and cheese.
4. Put 1/2 cup of filling on a tortilla; fold it and place it in a baking dish.
5. Top it with sauce, then cover and refrigerate it overnight.
6. Preheat the oven to 375°. Take out enchiladas from the refrigerator.
7. Bake it for 30 minutes while being covered.

8. Put the remaining cheese. Then bake while being uncovered till the point it is lightly brown.
9. Put toppings and serve.

3.4 Sausage Tortilla Breakfast Bake

Ingredients

- 1/2 cup tomatoes
- 1/2 green chiles
- 8 ounces turkey breakfast sausage
- 4 corn tortillas (8 inches)
- 1/4 cup pepper jack cheese, shredded
- 1/2 cup Monterey Jack cheese, shredded
- 2 green onions
- 3/4 cup milk, fat-free
- 6 eggs
- 3/4 tsp. paprika
- Sour cream
- 1/4 tsp. ground cumin
- Salsa, optional
- Green onions chopped, optional

Instructions

1. Preheat the oven to 350°. Take a skillet and cook sausage over the medium heat. Make sure its color is not pink anymore. Put tomatoes in it.
2. In a dish plate, place half of the tortillas. Put half of the mixture, green onions, and cheeses. Repeat this process while making layers.
3. Whisk eggs, paprika, milk, and cumin in a bowl. Then pour it over the layers.
4. Bake while keeping it uncovered for about half an hour.
5. Serve with green onions, sour cream, and salsa.

3.5 Egg Burritos

Ingredients

- 12 eggs
- 12 chopped bacon strips
- 1/2 tsp. salt
- 12 flour tortillas (6 inches)
- 1/4 tsp. pepper
- 1 1/3 cups cheddar cheese
- 4 thinly sliced green onions

Instructions

1. Take a skillet, and cook in it the bacon until it is crisp.
2. Whisk together salt, eggs, and pepper.
3. Over the medium heat, cook egg mixture in a skillet. Stir continuously till the eggs are cooked, and then remove the skillet from heat.
4. Pour 1/4 cup of egg mixture on each tortilla, and sprinkle with bacon, cheese, and green onions.
5. Make burritos, and serve.

3.6 Ramona's Chilaquiles

Ingredients

- 1/2 pound chorizo or pork sausage
- 1/2 pound ground beef
- 1 onion, chopped
- 1 can tomatoes
- 1 minced garlic clove
- 1 cup Monterey Jack cheese, shredded
- 6 ounces tortilla chips
- Chopped cilantro

For Topping:

- Diced avocado
- Sour cream
- Red onion, sliced

Instructions

1. Preheat the oven to 350°.
2. Take a skillet, and cook chorizo and beef with garlic and onion over the medium heat.
3. Stir in tomatoes and bring it to boil.
4. Take a greased baking dish and layer half of the beef mixture, 2 cups of chips, and 1/2 cup of cheese. Repeat this in layers.
5. In the end, bake it while being uncovered till the point cheese is melted.
6. Serve with toppings on it.

3.7 Huevos Rancheros with Tomatillo Sauce

Ingredients

- 2 tbsp. chopped onion
- 5 tomatillos, cut in half
- 1 serrano pepper
- 1 tsp. chicken bouillon granules
- 3 garlic cloves
- 1 can Southwestern black beans
- 1 cup Manchego cheese, shredded
- 8 eggs
- 8 tostada shells
- 1/2 cup sour cream

For Topping:

- Sliced avocado
- Chopped tomato
- Minced cilantro

Instructions

1. Finely chopped onion, the tomatillos, garlic, pepper, and bouillon, and set aside.
2. Take a saucepan, and cook the beans on low heat.
3. Break eggs into a skillet. Cover it and cook the eggs on low heat
4. Add cheese.
5. While serving, put beans over the tostada shells.
6. Put toppings of sour cream, tomatillo sauce, and eggs.
7. Garnish with avocado, tomato, and cilantro.

3.8 Avocado Quesadillas

Ingredients

- 1 mashed avocado
- 2 flour tortilla
- 50g cheddar cheese, grated

Instructions

1. Sprinkle half cheese on one tortilla wrap.
2. Spread the avocado on it.
3. Put the remaining cheese.
4.
5. Heat a pan over the medium heat. Put the quesadilla in it, and cook till the point it is golden brown.
6. Cook the other side of quesadilla by gently flipping it.
7. Serve hot!

3.9 Breakfast Tortas

Ingredients

- 3/4 cup black beans, refried
- 3 ciabatta rolls
- 1/4 cup sour cream

- 2 tsp. lime juice
- 1/4 cup fresh cilantro
- 4 drops chipotle pepper sauce
- 4 eggs
- 1/8 tsp. salt
- 1/2 cup Monterey Jack cheese, shredded
- 4 bacon strips, cooked and halved
- 1 tsp. olive oil
- 1/2 avocado, sliced
- 2 chopped green onions
- 1/3 cup salsa

Instructions

1. Cut one third from the top of each roll, and empty the bottom part.
2. Put roll bottoms on a baking sheet.
3. Take a bowl, mix sour cream, beans, lime juice, cilantro, salt, and chipotle pepper sauce.
4. Place 1/4 cup of this mixture inside each roll. Place an egg on it.
5. Bake it at 400° for almost 10 minutes.
6. Spread cheese over the eggs. Brush roll with olive oil and put it on the baking sheet.
7. Put toppings of avocado, bacon, salsa, and onions on each roll.
8. Replace the roll tops, and serve.

3.10 Mexican Baked Eggs

Ingredients

- 1 onion, chopped
- 1 1/2 tbsp. olive oil
- 1/3 tsp. chili flakes
- 2 tsp. cumin
- 1 tsp. paprika

- 450g kidney beans
- 1 large red capsicum, chopped
- 450g tomatoes, diced
- 4 eggs
- 1/2 cup water
- 1/3 cup coriander
- 1 avocado, sliced
- Salt, to season
- Pepper, to season
- Lime wedges, Sour cream, and tortillas, to serve

Instructions

1. Preheat the oven to 180°C. Take a pan and heat oil over the medium heat.
2. Put chili, onion, paprika, salt, cumin, and pepper, and cook for 5 minutes.
3. Add kidney beans, capsicum, water, and tomatoes in it.
4. After bringing it to boil, put the heat down, and cook for almost 10 minutes.
5. Put the mixture into four dishes. Fill them with each bean mixture, and put the egg.
6. Bake for 15-16 minutes.
7. Serve with sour cream, coriander, lime, avocado, and tortillas.

3.11 Breakfast Burrito Casserole

Ingredients

- 1/3 cup milk
- 8 eggs
- 1/2 tsp. salt
- 1 pound pork sausage
- 1/2 teaspoon pepper
- 1 cup sour cream
- 1 can chicken soup

- 6 flour tortillas (8 inches)
- 1 1/2 cups salsa
- 2/3 cup cheddar cheese, shredded
- 2/3 cup mozzarella cheese, shredded

Instructions

1. Preheat the oven to 350°. Mix milk, eggs, pepper, and salt.
2. Take a skillet, cook the egg mixture and stir it continuously over the medium heat till the point it is thickened.
3. Cook sausage in the same skillet, and keep the heat medium, then drain it.
4. Mix soup and sour cream together. Spread half mixture on a baking dish. Make a layer with half of the tortilla slices, scrambled eggs, half of the salsa, sausage. Then put the remaining sour cream mixture and tortillas.
5. Pour remaining salsa and cheeses.
6. Bake for almost 30-35 minutes while keeping it uncovered.
7. Serve with green onions and enchilada sauce.

3.12 Breakfast Tostada

Ingredients

- 1 tbsp. vegetable oil
- 4 slices bacon
- 15-ounces canned black beans
- Kosher salt and black pepper, to taste
- 4 tostada shells
- 1 egg
- 1/4 cup Cheddar cheese
- 1/4 avocado, diced
- 1 tbsp. sour cream
- 1 tbsp. salsa

- 1 tbsp. cilantro leaves

Instructions

1. Preheat oven to 400⁰ F.
2. Take a skillet, and cook the bacon over the medium heat till the point it is crisp.
3. Take a saucepan and keep the medium heat. Put vegetable oil, salt, black beans, and pepper. Mash the black beans.
4. Take a baking sheet and layer one tostada shell, one tbsp. Cheese and two tbsp. Beans. Repeat this with all layers of tostada shells. Bake till the point cheese is melted, and edges of tostadas start to turn into golden color.
5. Take a pan and heat oil over the medium heat.
6. Cook egg in it for about 5 minutes.
7. Put tostada on a plate, and top it with diced avocado, the fried egg, salsa, a remaining cheese, sour cream, and cilantro. Serve with bacon, and enjoy.

3.13 Mexican Sweet Potato Hash

Ingredients

- 1 1/2 tbsp. olive oil
- 2 pounds sweet potatoes
- 1 cup onion
- 1/2 cup bell pepper, green
- 1/2 cup bell pepper, red
- 3 cloves garlic
- 4 eggs
- 12 ounces soy chorizo

Instructions

1. Boil water in a pot, and add sweet potatoes to it. Boil till the point potatoes are tender. Then drain them and set aside.
2. Take a skillet and heat the oil over the medium heat. Add onion, red and green bell pepper in it. Saute it for almost 5 minutes
3. Add sweet potatoes and garlic. Saute for almost 4 minutes.
4. Add chorizo, and cook for almost 5 minutes.
5. Put the flame low and add eggs on the top of potato hash.
6. Cover it, and cook for 5 minutes
7. Serve and Enjoy!

3.14 Spicy Jalapeno Eggs and Sweet Pepper

Ingredients

- 4 slices sourdough
- 4 eggs
- 10 vine tomatoes
- 1 jalapeno
- 1 small sweet bell pepper, yellow, orange, or red
- 4 garlic cloves
- 2 tbsp. butter
- 1 tbsp. olive oil
- Salt, to taste
- Pepper, to taste
- Basil, for garnishing

Instructions

1. Preheat oven to the high broil.
2. Put tomatoes slices in an oven pan. Add salt, pepper, and olive oil. Then broil for almost 8 minutes.
3. Chop garlic. And add butter in it.

4. Spread mixture onto sourdough slices.
5. Cut jalapeno and sweet pepper.
6. When tomatoes are cooked, take the pan out of the oven and push tomatoes to the oven pan's edges.
7. Break eggs in the middle, and put the sliced jalapeno and pepper around eggs.
8. Add pepper and salt, and put it back for almost 6-8 minutes.
9. Put garlic slices of sourdough to toast.
10. Take a sourdough slice and top it with tomatoes, and egg.
11. Garnish it with basil, and serve.

3.15 Best-Ever Migas

Ingredients

- 6 corn tortillas
- 3 tbsp. of vegetable oil
- 1 jalapeño, chopped
- 1/2 onion, diced
- 3 cloves garlic, chopped
- 5 eggs
- 1/2 cups mild salsa
- Kosher salt, to taste
- 1/4 cups cilantro leaves
- 2 radishes, sliced
- 1 avocado, sliced
- 1/4 cups crumbled cotija cheese
- Hot sauce

Instructions

1. Take a pan and heat oil over the medium heat. Add corn tortillas in it, and cook for 5 minutes.
2. Put onion, garlic, and jalapeño in it, and cook for 4 minutes. Put the heat down to low.

3. Add eggs and salt.
4. Stir continuously till the point everything is mixed well.
5. Add salsa.
6. Top with radishes, cilantro, cheese, avocado, and hot sauce.
7. Serve and Enjoy!

Chapter 4: Mexican Lunch Recipes

Here are given some delicious and easy Mexican lunch recipes in this chapter. These recipes are fun to cook at home and perfect to enjoy with your family.

4.1 Prawn and Chorizo Quesadilla

Ingredients

- 1/2 red onion
- 1 tbsp. of olive oil
- 1 red pepper
- 1 garlic clove
- 70g chorizo, chopped
- 1 tbsp. of chipotle paste
- 1/2 tsp. coriander
- 1/2 tsp. cumin
- 2 flour tortillas
- 1 lime
- 100g prawns, chopped
- Guacamole, optional

Instructions

1. Take oil in a pan, and fry pepper and onion for almost 10 minutes.
2. Put the chorizo in it, and cook for another 5 minutes. Add the chipotle paste, garlic, cumin, prawns, and ground coriander, then cook for another 2 minutes.
3. Season with lime juice.
4. Put the mixture on a tortilla and place the second tortilla on it.
5. In a frying pan over high heat, add quesadilla and cook each side for almost 2 minutes.
6. Cut into pieces and serve.

4.2 Mexican-Style Stuffed Peppers

Ingredients

- 1 pound lean beef
- 4 red or green bell peppers
- 1 onion, diced
- 2 tsp. of chili powder
- 3 minced cloves garlic
- 1/2 tsp. cumin
- 1 can divided enchilada sauce
- 1 can tomatoes diced with peppers
- 2 cups of cheddar cheese
- 2 cups rice, cooked

Instructions

1. Preheat the oven to 375^0. Cut bell peppers into half. Put it in a baking dish.
2. Fry garlic, beef, and onion in a skillet. Pour in cumin, chili powder, diced tomatoes, and 2/3 cup enchilada sauce. Then let it simmer for 2-3 minutes.
3. Turn down the heat and add cooked rice in it.
4. Put beef mixture into the pepper. Add remaining cheese and enchilada sauce.
5. Bake while keeping uncovered till the point peppers and cheese is cooked. It might take around 30 minutes.
6. Put some taco toppings on it and serve.

4.3 Mexican Corn Salsa

Ingredients

- 1/4 cup minced red onion minced
- 2 cups fresh corn kernels
- 1/3 cups minced bell pepper, green or red
- 1/3 tsp. sea salt

- 2 1/2 lime juice
- 1 1/2 tbsp. fresh Jalapeño
- 3 tbsp. finely chopped cilantro
- Ground pepper

Instructions

1. Take a large bowl, and mix corn kernels, bell pepper, red onion, jalapeño, lime juice, cilantro, and salt.
2. Refrigerate it for about 24 hours to get the best taste.

4.4 Turkey Taco Lettuce Wraps

Ingredients

- 3/4 cup yellow onion, chopped
- 1 tbsp. of olive oil
- 1 pound ground turkey
- Salt, to taste
- Black pepper, to taste
- 3 cloves garlic
- 1/2 cup chicken broth
- 1/2 cup of tomato sauce
- 1 tsp. cumin
- 1 tbsp. of chili powder
- 1/2 tsp. of paprika

For Serving

- Iceberg or lettuce leaves
- Mexican cheese
- Roma tomatoes
- Red onion
- Avocado
- Cilantro
- Sour cream

Instructions

1. Heat the olive oil in a skillet.
2. Saute onion for 2 minutes. Then add garlic and turkey, pepper, and salt. Cook for 5 minutes.
3. Then add cumin, chili powder, paprika, chicken broth, and tomato sauce. Reduce the heat to simmer. Cook for 5 minutes.
4. Put the mixture on top of lettuce leaves, and serve with toppings of your choice.

4.5 Shrimp Enchiladas

Ingredients

- 1 bell pepper, red
- 1 1/2 tbsp. of olive oil
- 1/2 diced sweet onion
- 1 minced jalapeno
- Corn kernels
- 1 clove minced garlic
- 1 package seasoning mix
- 1 pound shrimp
- 1 can green chilies
- 1 package of Colby Jack cheese
- 1/2 cup of sour cream
- 10 corn tortillas
- 1 cup Monterey Jack cheese
- 2 cans enchilada sauce
- Fresh cilantro

Instructions

1. Preheat the oven to 350^0 and take a baking dish.
2. Take a skillet and heat oil over the medium heat. Add onion, red pepper, jalapeno, and corn. Cook until tender.

3. Add shrimp and garlic. Cook for almost 2 minutes. Then put taco seasoning mix in it, and cook.
4. Turn down the heat.
5. Add green chilies, Colby Jack cheese, and sour cream.
6. Put tortillas in the microwave for 30-35 seconds, till the point they are warm.
7. Place the mixture in the center of a tortilla, then roll it up. Put it in the baking dish.
8. Put enchilada sauce on the tortilla.
9. Add Monterey Jack cheese on top of it.
10. Bake for almost 30 minutes.
11. Take out and serve.

4.6 Mexican Quiche

Ingredients

- 6 ounces shredded cheddar cheese
- 1 pie crust, refrigerated
- 1 can tomatoes with green chilies
- 2 ounces black olives
- 1 can green chilies
- 3 eggs
- 1/2 tsp. of chili powder
- 1 cup of sour cream
- 1/2 tsp. paprika
- 1/8 tsp. cayenne pepper
- 1/4 tsp. cumin
- 1/8 tsp. garlic powder

Instructions

1. Place the pie crust on the pie plate.
2. Put cheddar over the bottom of the crust.
3. Then put tomatoes with green chilis and olives on it.

4. Mix eggs, chili powder, sour cream, paprika, cayenne, cumin, and garlic powder. Pour this mixture over the pie crust.
5. Bake at 350^0 for an hour.
6. Wait for 5 minutes to let it settle and then serve.

4.7 Grilled Cumin Lime Chicken

Ingredients

- 3-4 limes
- 3 chicken breasts
- 3 tbsp. olive oil
- 2 tsp. cumin
- 1 tbsp. kosher salt
- 2 tsp. black pepper
- 7 tbsp. vegetable oil
- 2-3 tbsp. salt

Instructions

1. Cut the chicken breast horizontally.
2. Put all chicken breast slices in a bowl. Add salt and put some water over chicken. Refrigerate it overnight for better taste.
3. Take it out and then pat dry it. Add lime juice and olive oil to it. Marinate the chicken and refrigerate it for another 3-7 hours.
4. Mix the ground pepper, cumin, and kosher salt in a bowl. Rub this mixture on the chicken.
5. Grill the chicken from each side.
6. Serve with chimichurri sauce and salsa.

4.8 Spicy Black Beans and Yellow Rice

Ingredients

For Beans

- 4 finely minced garlic cloves
- 3 tbsp. olive oil
- 1 small white onion
- 3 cups black beans, cooked
- 1 jalapeno, minced
- 1 tsp. of chili powder
- 2 1/2 cups vegetable stock
- 1/2 tsp. cumin powder
- 1/2 bell pepper, red

For Rice

- 1/2 tsp. turmeric
- 1 cup of rice
- 1/2 tsp. grated ginger
- Salt, to taste
- 1/4 tsp. coriander

Instructions

1. In a pot, heat olive oil, garlic cloves, and jalapeño pepper on low heat.
2. Then add chili powder, beans, 1/2 cup of stock, cumin, and cook for 25-35 minutes. In the end, add bell pepper and salt.
3. Add garlic cloves in the remaining olive oil
4. and heat them. Pour the remaining stock, bring it to boil. Add rice, reduce the heat, and cook for almost 15-20 minutes.
5. When rice is cooked, add spices.
6. Arrange black beans and rice on a serving platter.

4.9 Chicken Tostadas

Ingredients

- 3 tomatoes, diced
- 8 tostada shells or corn tortillas
- 4 avocados, diced
- 1/4 cup finely chopped cilantro
- 3 tbsp. finely chopped red onion
- 1 tsp. cumin
- 3/4 tsp. salt
- 1 tsp. of chili powder
- Lime juice
- 3 cups chicken, shredded
- 15 ounces can drained and rinsed black beans
- 1/2 cup Cotija or feta cheese

Instructions

1. For making tostada shells, arrange tortillas in a baking sheet, ad make a single layer. Bake each side at 400^0 for around 6 minutes.
2. Meanwhile, make guacamole salsa by mixing avocado, tomato, red onion, cumin, cilantro, chili powder, lime juice, and salt.
3. For assembly, put guacamole salsa, chicken, beans, and cheese on each shell.

4.10 Chicken, Cheese, and Chili Quesadillas

Ingredients

For Quesadillas:

- 6 ounces Colby, Monterey, Cheddar, or Jack cheese
- 12 corn tortillas
- 1 tbsp. jalapenos
- 4 tbsp. butter

- 1 cup chicken, cooked

For Salsa and Topping:

- 1/4 red onion
- 2 tomatoes
- 2-3 tbsp. cilantro
- Kosher salt
- Hot sauce, to taste
- 1 avocado, sliced

Instructions

1. Put tortillas on a surface, and equally divide the jalapenos, cheese, and the chicken.
2. Put remaining tortillas on the top and seal them gently.
3. Melt butter in a skillet. Fry both sides of quesadilla carefully. Make sure it does not burn. Add more butter if required.
4. In the meantime, prepare the salsa.
5. Take tomatoes, and cut them into halves. Peel off their skin. Then add onion, cilantro, salt, and hot sauce to taste.
6. Then, cut the quesadillas into 4 pieces.
7. Serve with avocado and salsa.

4.11 Refried Beans

Ingredients

- 1/2 cup onion
- 1 tbsp. olive oil
- 1/4 tsp. sea salt
- 1/2 tsp. of chili powder
- 2 cloves minced garlic
- 1/4 tsp. cumin
- 1/2 cup water
- 2 cans pinto beans

- 1 tbsp. lime juice, to taste
- 2 tbsp. chopped cilantro

Instructions

1. Heat the olive oil in a saucepan. Add salt and onions. Cook for 5-8 minutes.
2. Then add cumin, chili powder, and garlic. Stir constantly.
3. Add water and beans. Stir, and cook for about 5 minutes.
4. Lower the heat a little bit and use a masher to mash up beans.
5. Continue cooking, and often stir for some more minutes.
6. Add lime juice and cilantro.
7. Serve and Enjoy!

4.12 Mexican Lunch Loaf

Ingredients

- 2 tsp. baking powder
- 1 cup plain flour
- 1 tsp. Mexican chilli powder
- 2 tbsp. caster sugar
- 1 cup polenta
- 1 tsp. sea salt
- 125g can of corn kernels
- 1 red capsicum, diced
- 1/2 cup grated cheese
- 1 tbsp. finely chopped coriander leaves
- 3 onions, sliced
- 1 1/4 cups buttermilk
- 2 tbsp. olive oil
- 1 egg
- 1 red chilli, sliced

- Cherry tomatoes and Sliced avocado for serving

Instructions

1. Preheat the oven to 180^0 C, and grease a loaf pan.
2. Mix baking powder, chilli powder, and flour in a bowl.
3. Add sugar, polenta, salt, corn, capsicum, onion, cheese, and coriander.
4. Add pepper. Make space at the center.
5. Put buttermilk, oil, and egg in it. Transfer this mixture to the pan, and top it with sliced chilli.
6. Bake for almost 1 hour.
7. Make slices and serve with cherry tomatoes and avocado.

Chapter 5: Mexican Dinner Recipes

In this chapter, you will have some amazing, tasty, and fresh Mexican dinner recipes. Enjoy cooking, and have fun with an exciting mix of flavors.

5.1 Chicken and Bean Enchiladas

Ingredients

- 2 sliced red onion
- 1 tbsp. rapeseed oil
- 2 sliced red peppers
- 2 tsp. chipotle paste
- 2 crushed garlic cloves
- 2 chicken breasts
- Chopped coriander, a small bunch
- 500ml passata
- 400g can kidney beans or black beans
- 1 tsp. sugar or ketchup
- 50g cheddar, grated
- 6 tortillas
- Green salad, for serving

Instructions

1. Heat the oven to 200^{0}C.
2. Heat oil in a pan. Add peppers, onions, and garlic.
3. Then, cook for around 15 minutes.
4. Add the chipotle paste, and fry for 2 minutes.
5. Add chicken, and cook.
6. Add coriander, beans, and 140 ml of passata, then turn down the heat.
7. Pour remaining passata, ketchup, and the crushed garlic.
8. Put the mixture over the tortillas, and fold its sides, and roll it up.

9. Put the passata in a baking dish, and put enchiladas on the top.
10. Pour the remaining sauce, then add grated cheese.
11. Bake it for around 25-30 minutes.
12. Serve and Enjoy!

5.2 Cheesy Mexican Cauliflower Rice

Ingredients

- 1 chopped onion
- 1 tbsp. olive oil
- 2 cloves crushed garlic
- 1/2 tsp. cumin
- 1 tsp. oregano, dried
- 65 g cauliflower, grated
- Black pepper, to taste
- Salt, to taste
- 1 tbsp. tomato pureé
- 1 can black beans
- 250 g rotisserie chicken, shredded
- 175 g sweetcorn
- 2 thinly sliced jalapeños
- 200 g tomatoes
- 5 g coriander, freshly chopped
- 100 g Monterey jack cheese, grated
- 100 g cheddar cheese, grated
- Lime wedges, to serve

Instructions

1. Heat oil in a skillet over the medium heat.
2. Put the onion in it and cook for around 5 minutes.
3. Then add oregano, garlic, and cumin. Cook for 1 minute.
4. Add cauliflower in a dishtowel and drain any excess liquid.

5. Add more oil if required, and add grated cauliflower, pepper, and salt. Stir occasionally while cooking.
6. Add the tomato paste, black beans, chicken, tomatoes, corn, coriander, and jalapenos.
7. Add cheeses over it, then cover and cook until it melts.
8. Serve and Enjoy!

5.3 Chicken Fajitas

Ingredients

For Chicken:

- Salt, to taste
- 1 1/4 pounds chicken breasts
- 2 tbsp. olive oil
- 3 bell peppers, different colors
- 1 onion

For Marinade:

- 3 tbsp. olive oil
- 2 tbsp. lime juice
- 1 minced garlic clove
- 1/2 tsp. ground cumin
- 1/2 tsp. salt
- 1/2 tsp. chili powder
- 1/4 cup cilantro, chopped
- 1/2 minced jalapeño

For Serving:

- Salsa
- 10 flour tortillas
- Sliced avocado
- Iceberg lettuce
- Sour cream

Instructions

1. Cut chicken breasts into slices horizontally.
2. Mix together all the ingredients. Then put the chicken in it to marinate and mix well. Marinate for up to 9-10 hours in the refrigerator.
3. Take the chicken out, and sprinkle salt on the chicken slices.
4. Heat oil in a frying pan, and heat chicken for around 2-3 minutes on high heat. Turnover and cook the other side until it is well seared.
5. Cover seared breasts with foil then set aside.
6. Cook the onions and peppers on high heat. Spread the peppers and onions in the pan for around 2 minutes.
7. Put vegetables and cook for 2-3 minutes.
8. Cut chicken pieces, and serve with warm tortillas, onions and peppers, shredded cheese, guacamole, salsa, and iceberg lettuce, whatever you like.

5.4 Mexican Lasagna

Ingredients

- 1 can refried beans
- 2 pounds beef
- 1 can green chilies, chopped
- 2 tbsp. hot salsa
- 1 envelope of taco seasoning
- 12 ounces lasagna noodles, uncooked
- 1 jar mild salsa
- 4 cups Monterey Jack cheese, shredded
- 2 cups of water
- 1 can ripe olives, sliced
- 2 cups of sour cream
- 1 chopped tomato
- 3 chopped green onions

Instructions

1. Preheat the oven to 350°.
2. Take a skillet, and cook beef over the medium heat.
3. Add beans, chilies, hot salsa, and taco seasoning.
4. In a baking dish, put meat mixture and 1/3 of noodles. Add one cup of cheese. Then, repeat these layers twice.
5. Add water and salsa. Cover it and bake for around one hour.
6. Add sour cream, onions, olives, tomatoes, and the remaining cheese. Bake it while keeping it uncovered for 5 minutes.
7. Cut and server.

5.5 Slow-Cooker Enchiladas

Ingredients

- 1 can black beans
- 1 pound beef
- 1 cup frozen, roasted, or canned corn kernels,
- 1 can chopped green chiles
- 1 cup salsa,
- 2 tsp. taco seasoning mix
- 4 flour tortillas
- 1 can enchilada sauce
- 2 cups Mexican blend cheese, shredded

For Serving

- 1 diced tomato
- 1 diced avocado
- 2 tbsp. chopped cilantro leaves

Instructions

1. Take a skillet and heat oil over the medium heat. Then, add beef and cook for 3-5 minutes. Crumble the beef, and drain any excess fat, then turn down the heat.

2. Add corn, black beans, green chiles, salsa, enchilada sauce, and taco seasoning.
3. Coat the slow cooker from inside with a nonstick spray. Then put one tortilla in a slow cooker.
4. Place one-third of beef mixture on top of it, and sprinkle with a half cup of cheese. Repeat this with two more layers.
5. Put tortilla, cheese, and enchilada sauce.
6. Cook it on the low heat for around 3-4 hours.
7. Garnish with tomato, avocado, and cilantro.
8. Serve and Enjoy!

5.6 Garlic Beef Enchiladas

Ingredients

- 1 onion, chopped
- 1 pound beef
- 2 tbsp. all-purpose flour
- 1 tsp. salt
- 1 tsp. chili powder
- 1 tsp. garlic powder
- 1/4 tsp. rubbed sage
- 1/2 tsp. ground cumin
- 1 can stewed tomatoes

For Sauce:

- 5 minced garlic cloves
- 1/3 cup butter
- 1/2 cup of all-purpose flour
- 1 can tomato sauce
- 1 can beef broth
- 1 1/2 tbsp. chili powder
- 1 1/2 tsp. rubbed sage
- 1 1/2 tsp. ground cumin
- 1/2 tsp. salt

- 2 cups Monterey Jack cheese, shredded
- 10 flour tortillas

Optional Toppings:

- Fresh cilantro
- Grape tomatoes
- Chopped red onion
- Jalapeno peppers, sliced.

Instructions

1. Preheat the oven to 350°.
2. Take a skillet, and cook onion and beef over the medium heat.
3. Add seasonings and flour.
4. Stir in tomatoes and bring it to boil. Lower the heat, then simmer for 15 minutes.
5. Heat butter in a pan over the medium heat.
6. Cook garlic in it for around 1 minute. Mix flour, and blend it gradually.
7. Add broth, and bring it to boil. Cook for almost 2 minutes.
8. Add seasonings and tomato sauce.
9. Pour sauce into a baking dish. Place beef mixture on each tortilla.
10. Add cheese on top of it.
11. Top with some more sauce.
12. Bake it covered for around 30-35 minutes.
13. Then add the remaining cheese.
14. Bake it while keeping it uncovered till the point cheese is melted, 10-15.
15. Serve with your favorite toppings.

5.7 Roast Vegie Quesadillas

Ingredients

- 500g peeled sweet potato
- 1 red onion
- 1 tbsp. olive oil
- 150g broccoli
- 8 flour tortillas
- 240g mozzarella or cheddar, grated
- 85g sour cream
- 1-2 tbsp. pesto

Instructions

1. Preheat the oven to 200^{0}C. Put the onions and the sweet potato in a roasting pan, and drizzle it with season and oil.
2. Then roast it for 20 minutes.
3. Put broccoli to a pan. Mix the veggies, and roast them for another 10 minutes.
4. Take a frying pan and heat the oil over the medium heat.
5. Put one tortilla in the pan. Add 1/8 of the cheese. Then add 1/4 of the veggie mixture.
6. Add another 1/8 of the cheese. Put another tortilla on it, and seal it.
7. Cook it for around 1-2 minutes
8. Turn it and cook for another 1-2 minutes. Repeat this with all remaining tortillas, veggies, and cheese.
9. Mix pesto and sour cream in a bowl. Make pieces of quesadillas, and serve with pesto cream.

5.8 Corn, Black Bean, and Spinach Enchiladas

Ingredients

For Sauce:

- 1/4 cup of tomato paste
- 3 cups of vegetable broth
- 1/4 cup of all-purpose flour
- 2 tsp. cumin
- 2 tbsp. of olive oil
- 1/4 tsp. garlic powder
- 1/4 tsp. chili powder
- 1/4 tsp. onion powder
- Salt, to taste
- Pepper, to taste

For Enchiladas:

- 1 1/2 cups corn
- 15 ounces can black beans
- 6 ounces fresh spinach
- 1/3 cup cilantro
- 6 green onions
- 2 tsp. cumin
- 8 flour tortillas
- 1 cup vegan cheese, shredded

Instructions

1. Heat the oil in a skillet over the medium heat.
2. Put in tomato paste, cumin, flour, onion powder, garlic powder, and chili powder, and cook for one minute.
3. Add broth, and bring it to boil. Cook for 8-10 minutes until it gets slightly thickened.
4. Add pepper and salt to taste and put it aside.
5. Put spinach in a pan and heat for 2 minutes over the medium heat.

6. Take a bowl, and mix black beans, vegan cheese, wilted spinach, green onions, corn, cilantro, and cumin.
7. Preheat the oven to 375^{0}C. Spray a baking dish, and add some sauce to the bottom.
8. Fill tortillas with the mixture, and roll-up.
9. Pour the remaining sauce on top of enchiladas.
10. Add 1/4 cup of cheese on the top.
11. Bake it for 20 minutes, garnish with green onions and cilantro.
12. Serve and Enjoy!

5.9 Zucchini and Cheese Quesadillas

Ingredients

- 4 flour tortillas
- 2 cups zucchini
- 3/4 cup Cotija cheese, Monterey Jack, or shredded cheddar
- 1 jalapeño chile, sliced
- 2/3 cup scallions
- 1 1/3 tbsp. olive oil
- 3/4 cup tomato salsa
- 1 diced avocado
- Lime wedges, to serve

Instructions

1. Put half of the zucchini in between two tortillas. Top it with half of the cheese.
2. Then add the remaining cheese and zucchini.
3. Sprinkle half of the scallions and chile.
4. Put the remaining two tortillas on top of it, and seal it gently.
5. Take a nonstick skillet and heat oil over the medium heat. Then brush the pan with one teaspoon of oil.

6. Put one quesadilla in the pan and cook until it is golden brown.
7. Brush the top with one teaspoon of more oil and flip the quesadilla.
8. Repeat this with the second quesadilla.
9. Cut out quesadillas into pieces.
10. Add remaining scallions, avocado and chile. Then serve with lime and salsa.

5.10 Mushroom Quesadillas

Ingredients

- 1 pound mushrooms, thickly sliced
- 2 tbsp. olive oil
- 1 finely chopped clove garlic
- 1/4 tsp. salt
- 1/2 thinly sliced bunch scallions
- 1/8 tsp. black pepper
- Cilantro leaves
- 1 1/2 cups grated cheddar and Monterey Jack
- 10 corn tortillas

For Serving:

- Salsa

Instructions

1. Heat the oil in a skillet over the medium heat the oil.
2. Put mushrooms in the pan. Cook for 5 minutes.
3. Put scallions and garlic to the pan. Cook for 2-4 minutes, then add pepper and salt.
4. Place one tortilla in a pan and add 2 tablespoons mushrooms and cheese. Add 2 tablespoons more cheese and cilantro leaves.
5. Put one more tortilla on the top and seal it lightly.
6. Cook both sides and repeat this with all tortillas, filling, and cheese.

7. Cut all quesadilla into pieces.
8. Serve hot with salsa and jalapeño peppers.

Chapter 6: Mexican Soup Recipes

Cook and enjoy some of the most satisfying Mexican soup recipes given in this chapter to satisfy your cravings.

6.1 Chicken Tortilla Soup

Ingredients

- 1 onion, diced
- 2 tbsp. vegetable oil
- 2 tbsp. minced garlic
- 6 cups chicken broth
- 2 finely diced jalapenos
- 14.5 ounces can diced tomatoes
- 3 chicken breasts
- 14.5 ounces can black beans
- Salt, to taste
- Black pepper, to taste
- 2 limes
- 1 cup Monterrey cheese, shredded
- 8-inch tortilla
- 1 cup cilantro leaves, roughly chopped
- 1 sliced avocado

Instructions

1. Take a saucepan and heat the oil.
2. Add onions. Cook for around 2 minutes.
3. Add jalapenos and garlic.
4. Add tomatoes, chicken broth, and beans to the pot. Bring it to boil.
5. Lower the heat and add chicken breasts, and cook for 20-25 minutes.
6. When it is cook, take it out and let it cool so you could easily shred it.

7. Add fresh cilantro and lime juice.
8. Take a bowl and add shredded chicken in it. Pour soup over it.
9. Put a grilled tortilla, lime wedge, cheese, and avocado slices on top, and serve.

6.2 Chicken Enchilada Soup

Ingredients

- 1/2 cup chopped onion
- 2 tsp. of olive oil
- 3 cloves minced garlic
- 8 ounces can tomato sauce
- 3 cups chicken broth
- Chipotle chili, to taste
- 15 ounces can black beans
- 1/4 cup cilantro, chopped
- 14.5 ounces can diced tomatoes
- 1 tsp. cumin
- 2 chicken breasts
- 2 cups of frozen corn
- 1/2 tsp. oregano

For Topping:

- 1/4 cup scallions, chopped
- 3/4 cup cheddar cheese, shredded
- 1/4 cup cilantro, chopped
- 6 tbsp. sour cream
- 1 small avocado, diced

Instructions

1. Take a saucepan and heat oil over the medium heat.
2. Put garlic and onion and cook for 3-4 minutes.
3. Add chipotle adobo sauce, tomato sauce, and chicken broth, and bring it to boil.

4. Put cilantro in it and turn down the heat.
5. Add diced tomatoes, oregano, drained beans, cumin, corn, and stir.
6. Put chicken breasts, and cook for 5-6 hours on the low heat.
7. Shred the chicken and put it back to the soup.
8. Add cumin and salt to taste.
9. Pour in bowls and put avocado, cheese, cilantro, sour cream, tortilla chips, and scallions. Enjoy!

6.3 Burrito Bowl Soup

Ingredients

- 1 large onion, diced
- 2 tbsp. of canola oil
- 2 garlic cloves, minced
- 15 ounces canned tomatoes
- 1 tbsp. of cumin
- 15 ounces canned black beans
- 6 cups of chicken broth
- 2 cups of frozen corn
- 15 ounces green chile sauce
- 2 cups of mozzarella
- 1 cups of white rice
- Kosher salt to taste
- Chopped avocado

For Serving:

- Hot sauce
- Crushed tortilla chips
- Sour cream

Instructions

1. Take a large pot and heat oil over the medium heat.

2. Put garlic cloves and onion in it and cook for 6-8 minutes.
3. Put cumin.
4. Add black beans, frozen corn, and tomatoes. Stir constantly.
5. Add green chile sauce, chicken broth, and white rice in it and bring it to boil.
6. Lower the heat and cook while keeping it covered.
7. Stir constantly. When rice is tender, add mozzarella in it. Cook until it is melted.
8. Add salt and put avocado, hot sauce, tortilla chips, and sour cream on the top.

6.4 Hominy Beef Chili

Ingredients

- 1 beef chuck
- 2 tbsp. of canola oil
- 1 can hominy
- 1 can diced tomatoes
- 1 can beef broth
- 1 finely chopped sweet red pepper
- 1 can green chiles, chopped
- 1/2 cup onion, chopped
- 2 minced garlic cloves
- 1 tbsp. chili powder
- 1 tbsp. paprika
- 2 tsp. ground cumin
- 1/2 tsp. pepper
- 1/2 tsp. salt
- 1 1/2 cups of frozen corn

Instructions

1. Take a skillet and heat the oil in a pan over the medium heat.

2. Add beef in it.
3. Stir in broth, hominy, red pepper, tomatoes, onion, garlic, chiles, and seasonings.
4. Cover it and cook for almost 6-7 hours on low heat.
5. Mix corn and cook.
6. Serve with sour cream and cheese, and Enjoy!

6.5 Mexican White Chili

Ingredients

- 3 tbsp. olive oil
- 3 pounds of chicken breast
- 2 1/2 tbsp. chile powder
- Salt, to taste
- 3 tbsp. cumin
- Cayenne pepper, to taste
- 3 tbsp. minced garlic
- 3 cups of chopped onion
- 1 can of white beans
- 2 tsp. oregano
- 6 cups cheese, shredded
- 1 can green chiles, chopped
- 4-6 cups of chicken broth
- 2 cups of sour cream

For Garnishing:

- Sour cream
- Cilantro leaves, chopped
- Scallions, chopped
- Hot sauce
- Monterey Jack or Shredded cheddar cheese

Instructions

1. Preheat oven to 350°F.

2. Put the chicken in a pan. Add olive oil and chili powder, cumin, salt, and a pinch of cayenne in it.
3. Roast them for half an hour. Shred the chicken pieces and set aside.
4. Take a pot and heat the remaining olive oil. Put garlic and onion, and cook for 5 minutes.
5. Add shredded chicken, beans, oregano, chilies, chile powder, cumin, salt, and cayenne.
6. Add chicken broth.
7. Stir and simmer for 20 minutes on low heat.
8. Remove the pan from heat and set aside for 5 minutes.
9. Add cheese to the pot, and stir in sour cream.
10. Bring the pan back to simmer on low heat.
11. Cook chili for another 15-20 minutes. Add texture by using a masher to mash beans and the chicken.
12. Stir to mix everything.
13. Garnish and serve.

6.6 Mexican Corn and Chorizo Soup

Ingredients

- 1 onion, chopped
- 3/4 pound chorizo or pork sausage
- 1 chopped sweet red pepper
- 3 minced garlic cloves
- 1 chopped poblano pepper
- 1/3 cup flour
- 1/2 tsp. salt
- 1 tsp. ground cumin
- 1/2 tsp. pepper
- 1 1/2 pounds of potatoes
- 1/2 cup of sour cream
- 2 cartons of chicken broth
- 3 cups of frozen corn

Instructions

1. In a pan, cook chorizo over the medium heat for around 4-6 minutes. Crumble it and remove chorizo from pan to paper towels.
2. Put onion, poblano, and red peppers in the pan, and saute over the medium heat for 8-10 minutes.
3. Put garlic in it, and cook for 1 minute.
4. Mix seasonings and flour and cook for 3 minutes.
5. Add broth, and stir constantly.
6. Add corn and potatoes, and bring it to boil.
7. Lower the heat, and cook while keeping it uncovered.
8. When potatoes are cooked, add chorizo and sour cream.
9. Serve with cilantro and cheese.

6.7 Turkey Posole

Ingredients

- 2 yellow onions
- 3 tbsp. olive oil
- 2 poblano chile peppers
- 2 minced cloves garlic
- 4 cups of cooked turkey
- 2 quarts of turkey broth
- 1 can of green chile peppers, chopped
- 2 tbsp. dried oregano
- 1 tbsp. chili powder
- 2 cans cannellini beans
- 2 tbsp. ground cumin
- Salt, to taste
- Pepper, to taste

Instructions

1. Heat the oil over the medium heat.

2. Cook poblano chiles and onions in oil.
3. Put garlic.
4. Mix cumin, chile powder, and oregano.
5. Add cooked turkey, turkey broth, green chile peppers, hominy, and cannellini beans.
6. Add water if needed at this stage.
7. Add salt and pepper. Then bring it to boil.
8. Lower the heat, and simmer while keeping it covered for about one hour.
9. Take out in a bowl and serve.

6.8 Chunky Taco Soup

Ingredients

- 1 chopped medium onion
- 1 1/2 pounds beef
- 1 tbsp. olive oil
- 2 cans diced tomatoes with green chiles
- 2 cans pinto beans
- 2 cups of water
- 1 can of corn
- 1 can of black beans
- 1 envelope of salad dressing mix
- 1/4 cup of minced cilantro
- 1 envelope of taco seasoning

Instructions

1. Take a pan and heat onion and beef and onion in the oil.
2. Put tomatoes, pinto beans, black beans, water, salad dressing mix, corn, and taco seasoning. Then bring it to boil. Lower the heat. Simmer while keeping it covered for about 20-30 minutes.
3. Add cilantro, and serve.

6.9 Mexican Meatball Soup

Ingredients

- 1 chopped red onion
- 1 tbsp. cooking oil
- 2 jalapeño peppers, chopped
- 2 1/4 tsp. dried oregano
- 1 zucchini, diced
- 1/2 tsp. ground cumin
- 2 cups of water
- 1 quart of canned chicken broth
- 1 1/2 cups of canned tomatoes
- 3/4 tsp. black pepper
- 1 3/4 tsp. salt
- 1/2 pound beef, grounded
- 2 1/2 tsp. bread crumbs
- 2 cloves minced garlic
- 1 egg
- 1 tbsp. lime juice
- 1 cup corn kernels

Instructions

1. Heat the oil in the pot over the low heat.
2. Add the onion in it with half of the jalapeños. Cook for about 5 minutes.
3. Put zucchini, cumin, dried oregano, and cook for almost 3 minutes.
4. Then add the water, broth, tomatoes, salt, and black pepper. Then simmer it for about 15 minutes.
5. Take a bowl, mix beef, the remaining jalapeño, garlic, cumin, dried oregano, salt, black pepper, egg, and the bread crumbs. Make meatballs.
6. Put corn and meatballs to the soup, and then simmer for about 5 minutes.

7. Add lime juice and fresh oregano, and serve.

6.10 Mexican Black Bean Soup

Ingredients

- 1 diced red capsicum
- 1 tbsp. olive oil
- 1 finely chopped brown onion
- 1 tsp. ground cumin
- 1 finely chopped garlic clove
- Pinch of chili flakes, dried
- 400g can of diced tomatoes
- 3 cups of vegetable stock
- 1 cup corn kernels, frozen
- 1 tbsp. lime juice
- 425g can o black beans
- 1 packet of corn chips
- 1/2 avocado
- 1/4 cup chopped coriander leaves
- 80g crumbled fetta

Instructions

1. Take a pan and heat the oil.
2. Put onion and capsicum in a pan. Cook for 5 minutes, and stir constantly.
3. Put cumin, garlic, and chili in it.
4. Then add tomatoes, stock, beans, and corn. Bring it to simmer. Then lower the heat.
5. Add lime juice, and season it with pepper and salt.
6. Sprinkle corn chips, avocado, coriander, and fetta.

6.11 Mexican Sweet Potato Soup

Ingredients

- 1 finely chopped onion
- 1 tbsp. of vegetable oil
- 1 tbsp. of chipotle paste
- 750g sweet potato
- 1 cube of vegetable stock
- Coriander leaves
- 4 bread rolls

Instructions

1. Take a pan and heat the oil.
2. Put the onion in it and cook for 4-5 minutes.
3. Add chipotle paste.
4. Add stock cube in boiling water, and then add it to the pan.
5. Add sweet potatoes. Then bring it to boil. Simmer it while keeping it covered for about 10 minutes. Use a blender to make it smooth.
6. Take out in a bowl. Sprinkle coriander leaves and bread rolls, and serve.

Chapter 7: Vegetarian Mexican Recipes

Here are given the most delicious vegetarian Mexican recipes in this chapter. Try these cuisines for having perfect plant-based food in your menu, and enjoy!

7.1 Mexican Fiesta Rice

Ingredients

- 1 finely chopped onion
- 2 tbsp. of olive oil
- 2 peppers, finely chopped
- 1 tsp. of cumin seeds
- 1/2 tsp. of ground cumin
- 4 finely chopped garlic cloves
- 1 tbsp. of tomato purée
- 250g of rice
- Paprika, a small pinch
- 450ml vegetable stock
- Coriander, finely chopped for serving
- Sliced onions, for serving

Instructions

1. Take a skillet, and heat oil, and add the pepper, onion, cumin, and garlic—sizzle for 8-10 minutes.
2. When the vegetables are golden and soft, add tomato purée and paprika, then cook for about 1 min.
3. Add rice.
4. Pour stock in it, then cover. Bring it to boil.
5. Lower the heat, then cook for around 10 minutes.
6. Turn down the heat and keep it covered for another 10 minutes.
7. To serve immediately, add spring onions and coriander.

8. To serve it later, cool down the rice, then refry it before serving. Then add spring onions and coriander.

7.2 Mexican Tomato Rice

Ingredients

- 1 onion, peeled and chopped
- 1 can of peeled tomatoes
- 2 cups chicken broth
- 1/2 tsp. ground cumin
- 1 1/2 tsp. kosher salt
- 1/3 cup cooking oil
- 1 to 2 chile peppers, minced
- 2 cups of white rice
- 4-5 finely chopped cloves garlic
- Juice of 2 limes
- Lime wedges, to serve
- 1/4 cup of finely chopped cilantro

Instructions

1. Place onion and the tomatoes in a blender, and blend it until it is smooth.
2. Add 2 cups of this mixture to a saucepan.
3. Add salt, chicken broth, and cumin. Bring it to boil over the medium heat.
4. On the other hand, toast rice.
5. Over medium heat, heat the oil until shimmering.
6. Put rice and cook, stirring frequently. When it is golden and lightly toasted, put jalapeños in it, and cook for about 2 minutes.
7. Lower the heat. And add garlic, then cook for around 30 seconds.
8. Put boiling tomato puree on the rice and mix thoroughly.

9. Lower the heat. Then cover it and cook. When the liquid is fully absorbed, and rice is cooked, turn off the heat.
10. Set aside for 10 minutes. Put lime juice and cilantro and mix it.
11. Season it with salt if needed, then serve.

7.3 Black Bean Tostadas

Instructions

- 1/2 diced red onion
- 2 cans of black beans
- 1 bell pepper, green
- 1/2 tsp. chili powder
- 3 garlic cloves
- 1/4 tsp. paprika
- Cayenne pepper, a small pinch
- 1/2 tsp. cumin
- Salt, to taste
- 3-4 cup of vegetable stock
- Black pepper, to taste
- 1 tbsp. lime juice

For Tostadas:

2 3 tbsp. of olive oil

8 corn tortillas

For Topping:

- Shredded lettuce
- Avocado, sliced
- Grilled corn
- Cherry tomatoes
- Green onions
- Fresh cilantro

- Cotija cheese, crumbled
- Lime wedges

Instructions

1 Put the onion, black beans, garlic cloves, pepper, paprika, chili powder, cumin, salt, cayenne, and pepper to a pan over medium heat.
2 Mix lime juice and stock in it and stir.
3 Simmer beans while keeping it uncovered, and cook for 10-15 minutes. When the mixture starts to thicken, turn down the heat, and set aside.
4 Remove garlic cloves from it.
5 For making tostadas, fry them in a pan.
6 To do it, heat a pan over the medium heat. Add oil in it.
7 Put the tortilla in it, and cook for 1-2 minutes. Flip and cook the other side.
8 Drain out any excess oil from it, and add salt. Go through the same process for the remaining tortillas.
9 To serve, add some black bean mixture on the top of the tortilla. Add lettuce, pickled avocado onion, tomatoes, grilled corn, cotija cheese, cilantro, and green onions.
10 Sprinkle lime juice, serve, and enjoy!

7.4 Smoky Veggie Nachos

Ingredients

- 4 corn tortillas
- 1 tsp. smoked paprika
- 400g can of black beans
- 2 red peppers
- 1/2 bunch of finely chopped parsley
- 1 finely sliced jalapeño
- 50g of yogurt
- 4 finely sliced spring onions

- 1 avocado, peeled and chopped
- 4 tomatoes, finely chopped
- 1/2 bunch of finely chopped coriander
- 1 lime, juiced
- 1 finely grated garlic clove
- 1 tbsp. of rapeseed oil

Instructions

1. Preheat the oven to 180C.
2. Make pieces of the tortillas, and make triangles. Spread them over two baking sheets.
3. Put oil on it, then add paprika. Bake it for around 7-8 minutes. When it is crisp, leave it to cool down.
4. Heat grill over high heat, then grill peppers for around 7-10 minutes. Leave it to cool down, then peel it off. Toss it with parsley and the beans.
5. Combine all ingredients to make salsa.
6. Put nachos on a plate, and top it with salsa, the bean mix, jalapeño, and yogurt.
7. Pour some paprika, and serve.

7.5 Enchilada Pie

Ingredients

- 1/2 cup onion, diced
- 1 pound of ground beef
- 2 minced cloves garlic
- 1 can of green chilies
- 1 can of Tex Mex-style tomatoes
- 2 tbsp. fresh cilantro, chopped
- 1 can of refried black beans
- 1 packet of taco seasoning mix
- 2 cans of red enchilada sauce
- 1/2 cup of sour cream
- 2 cups of Monterey Jack cheese, shredded

- 2 cups of pepper jack cheese, shredded
- 8 flour tortillas

Instructions

1 Preheat the oven to 200 degrees C.
2 Cook onions and beef in a skillet over the medium heat for about 7-10 minutes.
3 Put garlic in it, and cook for about 30 seconds.
4 Add green chiles, diced tomatoes, taco seasoning mix, and cilantro. Remove it from the heat.
5 Take a bow, and add black beans and red enchilada sauce.
6 Mix Monterey Jack cheese and pepper jack cheese together in a bowl.
7 Heat a skillet over the medium heat, and cook tortillas in it. When they are crisp, take them out.
8 Put a tortilla in a pan, and spread a layer of black bean mixture, then a layer of beef mixture.
9 Add 1 cup of cheese mixture and 1/4 cup of red enchilada sauce on top of it.
10 Repeat this process for all tortillas.
11 Cover the pan with an aluminum foil. Bake in the oven until the enchiladas are cooked, and the cheese is bubbling. It will take around 40 minutes.
12 Cool it down for around 15 minutes.
13 Serve it with sour cream.

7.6 Easy BBQ beans

Ingredients

- 2 cups of Barbecue Sauce
- 15 ounces can of pinto or cannellini beans
- 1 chopped green bell pepper
- 1–2 tsp. of liquid smoke
- 1 chopped yellow onion

Instructions

1 Preheat a saucepan over the medium heat.
2 Then drain and rinse the beans.
3 Put bell pepper, onion, and 2-3 tbsp. of veggie stock or water for cooking.
4 Cook it for about 3-4 minutes.
5 Lower the heat. Then add beans, liquid smoke, and BBQ Sauce.
6 Stir constantly until the beans are coated thoroughly.
7 Simmer it for around 10-15 minutes, then turn off the heat.
8 Serve and enjoy!

7.7 Vegetarian Mushroom Fajitas

Ingredients

- 1 1/2 cups of fresh mushrooms
- 2 bell peppers, red
- 1 sliced onion
- 1/2 tsp. of curry powder
- 1 tbsp. of olive oil
- 1/2 tsp. of chili powder
- 4 flour tortillas
- 1/4 tsp. of cumin
- Sour cream, optional

Instructions

1 Heat mushrooms, the peppers, and the onion in the olive oil for 3-5 minutes.
2 Put spices in it, and cook for about 2 minutes. Make sure the veggies are tender.
3 Put some mixture on a tortilla, the top sour cream over it.
4 Serve and enjoy!

7.8 Grilled Mexican Street Corn

Ingredients

- 1/2 cup of mayonnaise
- 4 ears yellow corn
- 2 tbsp. of finely chopped cilantro
- 1 small pinch of cayenne pepper
- 1 minced clove garlic
- 1 cup of Cotija cheese, finely crumbled
- Lime wedges, to serve
- 1/2 tsp. of chili powder

Instructions

1. Heat a grill over the medium heat.
2. Meanwhile, take a bowl, mix mayonnaise, garlic, cilantro, and cayenne pepper.
3. Put cotija cheese in a dish.
4. When the grill is heated, put corn on the grill. Leave space between corns.
5. Let it cook over grill. Make sure to turn it over to cook from all sides.
6. Brush all corn sides with mayonnaise mixture.
7. Roll it in cheese.
8. Take it out on a baking sheet or platter. Repeat this process with the remaining corn.
9. Add chili powder and cayenne pepper on all sides.
10. Sprinkle with cilantro and use lime wedges to serve.

7.9 Green Tomato Salsa

Ingredients

- ½ diced white onion
- 1 pound green tomatoes
- 1-2 thinly sliced Serrano peppers

- 1/2 cup of chopped cilantro
- 1 tbsp. of lime juice
- 1/2 tsp. of salt

Instructions

1. Cut tomatoes into quarters. Place them on a baking sheet having a foil.
2. Put the baking sheet in the oven. Broil them for 5 minutes.
3. Meanwhile, put the diced onions in a bowl. Fill it with cold water, and soak for 5-10 minutes.
4. Put the broiled tomatoes to a food processor, and break into pieces.
5. Remove water from onion and mix it with peppers, salt, lime juice, and cilantro. Then pulse it again until having the desired texture.
6. Season it with more lime juice and salt if needed.
7. Serve immediately, put it in the fridge for 1-2 hours for additional flavor.

7.10 Mexican Sweet Potatoes

Ingredients

- 2 sweet potatoes
- 1 tbsp. of olive Oil
- 1 diced sweet onion
- 1 chopped bell pepper, red
- 2 minced garlic cloves
- 2 cups of chopped mushrooms
- 1/2 cup of canned black beans
- 2 tbsp. of tomato taste
- 1/2 cup of frozen corn
- 1 tbsp. of chili powder
- Sea salt, to taste
- Black pepper, to taste

- 1 tsp. of ground cumin
- 1 mashed avocado
- Fresh cilantro, for garnishing
- 1 tbsp. sour cream or yogurt

Instructions

1 Preheat the oven to 200 degrees celcius. Prepare a baking sheet with a paper.
2 Make pieces of sweet potatoes, and put them on the baking sheet.
3 Cook them for 15-18 minutes, then take it out of the oven.
4 Meanwhile, take a skillet, and heat the oil.
5 Put onion, garlic, and bell pepper in it. Cook for 4-5 minutes.
6 Add mushrooms. Cook for another 6-7 minutes.
7 Add corn, tomato paste, black beans, chili powder, and chili powder.
8 Put Mexican mixture on the sweet potatoes, and put mashed avocado and yogurt on the top of them.
9 Garnish with cilantro and enjoy!

Chapter 8: Mexican Salad Recipes

Try and enjoy easting some healthy, easy, and tasteful Mexican salad recipes given in this chapter.

8.1 Mexican Salad with Tortilla Croutons

Ingredients

- 1 tbsp. of olive oil
- 3 flour tortillas
- 1 tsp. of Mexican seasoning mix
- 400g can of black bean
- 1 shredded iceberg lettuce,
- 200g pack of cherry tomato
- Juice of 1 lime
- 2 sliced avocados
- 1/2 bunch of coriander leaves

Instructions

1. Heat the oven to 200 degrees Celsius. Put seasoning mix and oil on pieces of tortilla, and put it on the baking tray. Cook for around 10-12 minutes until it is crisped.
2. Take a bowl. Put tomatoes, beans, avocado, lime juice, and the iceberg in it.
3. Drizzle over the dressings and mix it thoroughly.
4. Sprinkle coriander and croutons on it, and serve.

8.2 Spicy Chicken, Jalapeño and Mango Salad

Ingredients

- 2 tbsp. of jalapeños, finely chopped
- 250g pack of sliced cherry tomato
- Small bunch of chopped coriander

- 1 finely chopped red onion
- Juice of 1 lime
- 1 tbsp. of olive oil
- 2 lettuces, cut into pieces
- 4 chicken breasts, cooked and torn into shreds
- 1 sliced red pepper
- A handful of tortilla chips
- 1 ripe diced mango

Instructions

1. Mix jalapeños, cherry tomatoes, lime juice, coriander, oil, and onion in a bowl. Add some seasoning.
2. Top with the remaining ingredients.
3. Mix to coat.
4. Put tortilla chips on the top of it,
5. Serve with lime wedges, and enjoy!

8.3 Mexican Bean Salad

Ingredients

- 1/2 cup red wine vinegar
- 1 can of drained kidney beans
- 1 can of drained black beans
- 1 can of cannellini beans
- 1 package of corn kernels, frozen
- 1 bell pepper, red
- 1 bell pepper, green
- 1 chopped red onion
- 1/2 cup of olive oil
- 2 tbsp. of lime juice
- 1 tbsp. of salt
- 1 tbsp. of lemon juice
- 2 tbsp. of white sugar
- 1 clove garlic, crushed

- 1/2 tbsp. of ground cumin
- 1/4 cup fresh cilantro, chopped
- 1/2 tbsp. of black pepper
- 1/2 tsp. of chili powder
- 1 dash pepper sauce

Instructions

1. Take a bowl, and mix bell peppers, beans, red onion, and frozen corn.
2. Take another bowl, mix red wine vinegar, olive oil, lemon juice, lime juice, salt, sugar, garlic, cumin, cilantro, and black pepper.
3. Season with chili powder and hot sauce.
4. Add olive oil over vegetables, and mix it well.
5. Chill before serving.
6. Enjoy your salad.

8.4 Mexican Corn Salad

Ingredients

- 4 cups corn kernels
- 1 tbsp. of butter
- Salt, to taste
- Pepper, to taste
- 1/4 cup of chopped red onion
- 1 finely chopped bell pepper, red
- 3 tbsp. of lime juice
- 1/2 cup of cilantro leaves, for garnishing
- 1/4 cup of sour cream
- 1/2 tsp. of cumin
- 2 tbsp. mayonnaise
- 1/4 tsp. smoked paprika
- 1/3 cup of finely grated cotija cheese
- 1/2 tsp. of chili powder

Instructions

1. Take a pan and heat butter over medium heat.
2. Put corn in the pan. Cook for around 3-5 minutes.
3. Season with pepper and salt to taste.
4. Cool the corn at room temperature.
5. Put it in a bowl with red bell pepper, jalapeno, onion, and chopped cilantro.
6. Take another bowl, mix cream, lime juice, mayonnaise, smoked paprika, cumin, and chili powder.
7. Put the dressing on the corn mixture.
8. Sprinkle with chili powder, cotija cheese, and cilantro.
9. Serve and Enjoy!

8.5 Mexican Chopped Salad

Ingredients

For Dressing:

- 2 tbsp. of honey
- 1/4 cup of lime juice
- 1/2 tsp. of cumin
- 1/2 tsp. of salt
- 1 finely minced clove garlic
- 2 tbsp. of canola oil
- Black pepper, to taste
- 2 tbsp. olive oil
- Salt, to taste

For Tortilla Strips:

- 1 1/2 tbsp. of canola oil
- 6 corn tortillas (6-inches)
- 1/2 tsp. sea salt

For Salad:

- 4 diced tomatoes

- 1 diced bell pepper, any color
- 1 head lettuce
- 1/2 diced red onion
- 1 diced zucchini
- 1 1/2 cups corn
- 1/2 diced jicama
- 1 1/2 cups of black beans
- 1 1/2 cups corn
- 1/2 cup cilantro, finely chopped

Instructions

1. To prepare the dressing, mix lime juice, cumin, honey, salt, and garlic.
2. Gradually pour the oils while stirring it continuously.
3. Season to taste and put more pepper and salt, if required. Then set it aside.
4. Preheat the oven to 400 degrees F to get it ready for preparing tortilla strips.
5. Put tortillas on the cutting board, and cut them half.
6. Transfer the tortilla strips to a pan, then drizzle them with oil.
7. Add salt, then bake for around 15-20 minutes, while stirring it continuously until it is golden brown. Set aside.
8. To prepare the salad, put corn in the oven, the cook for almost 3 minutes.
9. Cut out the bottom of the corn, then pull back silks and husks and silks.
10. Cut corn kernels from the husks. Set them aside.
11. Mix other ingredients and corn in a bowl. Mix to combine.
12. Pour dressing and stir well.
13. Add cilantro leaves for garnishing.
14. Serve with the tortilla strips on the top.

8.6 Mexican Salad with Lime Dressing

Ingredients

For Salad:

- 1 cup tomatoes, halved
- 1 large head lettuce, chopped
- 1 diced avocado
- 1/2 yellow onion, sliced
- 1/2 sliced cucumber
- l cup peas, whole
- 1/3 bunch of fresh cilantro
- 1/2 cup of corn kernels, freshly cooked or canned

For Lime Dressing:

- 1/3 cup of lime juice
- 1/3 cup of olive oil
- Tabasco sauce, to taste
- 1/8 tsp. of black pepper
- 1/2 tsp. of sea salt

Instructions

1. Mix all ingredients for salad dressing and whisk together.
2. Chop all ingredients of the salad and mix it in a salad bowl.
3. Make sure to shake the dressing before serving.
4. Drizzle as much dressing on the salad as you like, and enjoy!

8.7 Spicy Mexican Salad

Ingredients

- 1 1/2 cups of shredded Monterey and Cheddar cheese
- 1 package of chopped lettuce

- 1 can of pinto beans
- 2 tomatoes, chopped
- 1 can of black beans
- 1 bag of corn chips
- 1 bottle of salad dressing

Instructions

1. Take a bowl, and combine cheese, romaine, pinto beans, tomatoes, and black beans.
2. Add corn chips and dressing, toss it well, and serve.

8.8 Mexican Avocado and Shrimp Salad

Ingredients

- 1 1/3 tbsp. olive oil
- 3/4 pound of shrimp
- 2 tbsp. of lime juice
- Salt, to taste
- Pepper, to taste
- 1/2 tsp. of honey
- 1 tsp.of chili powder
- 1/2 cup of corn kernels
- 1/2 cup of black beans, cooked
- 1 cup tomato, diced
- 1/2 thinly sliced avocado
- 1/3 cup cilantro, chopped
- 4 cups of mixed greens

Instructions

For Dressing:

1. Mix olive oil, lime juice, honey, and chopped cilantro.
2. Add pepper and salt.

For Black Bean Salsa:

1. Take a bowl, mix corn, black beans, tomato, cilantro, and lime juice. Add salt and mix it well.
2. Heat olive oil on the high heat.
3. Add chili powder, pepper, and salt to the shrimp. Cook each side for around 2-3 minutes. Make sure shrimp is opaque and pink.

Assemble the Salad:

Put the greens and dressing in a bowl. Add shrimp, avocado, and black bean salsa on the top, and serve.

8.9 Orange, Avocado, and Jicama Salad

Ingredients

- 2 tbsp. of lime juice
- 3 oranges
- 1 tbsp. cider vinegar
- 1 pinch cayenne pepper
- 2 tbsp. of olive oil
- 1/4 cup cilantro, chopped
- Salt, to taste
- Black pepper, to taste
- 2 thinly sliced avocados
- 1 jicama, peeled and sliced
- 1 cup of feta cheese, crumbled

Instructions

1. Squeeze oranges
2. To extract orange juice. Mix it with lime juice, oil, vinegar, and cayenne.
3. Add jicama, pepper, and salt. Set aside for about 15 minutes.
4. Add orange juice, avocado, cilantro, and feta.
5. Serve, and enjoy!

8.10 Mexican Black Bean and Chicken Salad

Ingredients

- 1 1/2 cups of chicken breast, cooked
- 6 cups of torn lettuce
- 1 can black beans
- 1/2 cup of shredded cheddar cheese
- 1 cup of green pepper, chopped
- 1 cup seeded tomatoes, chopped
- 1/2 cup red onion, sliced
- 1/4 cup seeded tomato, chopped
- 1/4 cup fresh cilantro, minced
- 1 tbsp. cider vinegar
- 1 tbsp. lime juice
- 1/4 tsp. chili powder
- 1 tbsp. olive oil
- 1/2 tsp. lime zest
- 1/4 teaspoon salt
- 1 minced garlic clove
- 1/4 tsp. pepper

Instructions

1. Take a large bowl, mix chicken, lettuce, beans, cheese, green pepper, tomatoes, and onion. Take a blender, and combine the ingredients for the vinaigrette.
2. Then cover it. Make sure it is smooth before pouring over the salad.
3. Serve and enjoy!

Chapter 9: Mexican Desserts

Try this fantastic collection of Mexican dessert recipes given in this chapter, and make your day.

9.1 Tres Leches Cake

Ingredients

- 1 tsp. baking powder
- 1 1/2 cups of flour
- 1/2 cup butter, unsalted
- 5 eggs
- 1 cup of white sugar
- 1/2 tsp. vanilla extract
- 1 can of condensed milk, sweetened
- 2 cups of whole milk
- 1 can of evaporated milk
- 1 cup of white sugar
- 1 1/2 cups of cream
- 1 tsp. of vanilla extract

Instructions

1. Put flour and grease on a baking pan, and preheat the oven to 175 C.
2. Mix baking powder and flour.
3. Mix cream butter and 1 cup of sugar until fluffy.
4. Put eggs and vanilla extract in it and beat well.
5. Gradually pour butter mixture to the flour mixture, mix well.
6. Bake it for around 30 minutes.
7. Mix condensed milk, and whole milk, and evaporated milk.
8. Put on the cake.

9. Mix whipping cream, remaining sugar, and remaining vanilla until it is thick. Pour on the cake.
10. Make sure to keep the cake in the refrigerator, enjoy!

9.2 Dulce de Leche

Ingredients

- 1 1/4 cups of sugar
- 4 cups of milk
- 1/4 tsp. of baking soda
- 1 tsp. of vanilla
- 1 can of sweetened condensed milk

Instructions

1. Mix milk, sugar, and baking soda in a saucepan. Bring it to boil, then lower the heat and keep it uncovered, stir until thickened.
2. Put vanilla into it, and let it cool.
3. Meanwhile, heat the oven to 425 degrees F.
4. Pour the can of sweetened condensed milk in a pie plate. Cover it tightly with a foil.
5. Put the plate in a pan and add hot water. Bake the milk in the oven for about 45 minutes. Regularly see the water level, and continue baking for another 45 minutes.
6. Remove the pie plate from water and let it cool.

9.3 Rumchata Cupcakes

Ingredients

For Cupcakes:

- 1 cup of Rumchata
- 1/2 cup of vegetable oil
- 1 box of vanilla cake mix

- 3 eggs

For Frosting:

- 1 cup of butter
- 4 cups of powdered sugar
- 1/3 cup of Rumchata
- 1 tsp. of cinnamon
- 1 tsp. of vanilla extract
- 1 pinch of kosher salt

Instructions

1. Put the cupcake wrappers on the cupcake pan, and preheat the oven to 350 C.
2. Mix ingredients until smooth.
3. Put batter into the liners, and bake for 25 minutes. Make sure the toothpick comes out clean. When ready, let it cool.
4. Mix 2 cups of powdered sugar with other ingredients. Mix well until creamy.
5. Add powdered sugar in it, and beat until fluffy and light.
6. Pour Rumchata frosting on the cupcakes.
7. Garnish with cinnamon sticks and cinnamon, and serve.

9.4 Churro Apple Pies

Ingredients

For the Apple Pie Filling:

- 2 tbsp. of fresh lemon juice
- 5 apples diced into pieces
- 1 1/4 of cup water
- 1 pinch nutmeg
- 1/2 cup of brown sugar
- 3 tbsp. of cornstarch

- 1 tsp. of ground cinnamon

For the Caramel Sauce:

- 1/4 cup of butter
- 1 cup of brown sugar
- 1/2 cup of thickened cream

Instructions

1. Mix apples with lemon juice in a saucepan.
2. Whisk water and cornstarch until it is lump-free.
3. Put the mixture into a saucepan over the medium heat.
4. Add brown sugar, nutmeg, and cinnamon.
5. Mix to combine it well. Bring it to boil. Whisk continuously.
6. When the mixture starts to thicken, put the diced apple in it.
7. Lower the heat and cover the pan.
8. Let it cook for around 8-10 minutes until soft.
9. Turn down the heat while keeping it covered, and let it cool.
10. Fill each churro bowl with apple pie filling.
11. Drizzle ice cream and caramel sauce.
12. To prepare caramel sauce, mix heavy cream and brown sugar into a saucepan over the medium heat. When sugar just starts to melt, put butter in it.
13. Lower heat and continue cooking until sauce thickens.
14. Let it cool, then pour onto the Apple Pie Churros.
15. Server and enjoy!

9.5 Mexican Hot Chocolate Pie

Ingredients

For the Crust:

- 2 tbsp. of sugar
- 1 1/2 cups of cracker crumbs, divided

- 1 tsp. of ground cinnamon
- 2 tbsp. of egg white
- 1/8 tsp. salt
- 2 tbsp. of butter

For the Filling:

- 2 tbsp. of cornstarch
- 1/2 cup of sugar
- 1 tbsp. of unsweetened cocoa
- 1/8 tsp. salt
- 1/4 tsp. of espresso granules
- 1/8 tsp. of red pepper
- 1 egg yolk
- 1 egg
- 1 3/4 cups of 2% milk
- 1 1/2 cups of frozen topping
- 2 ounces of chopped dark chocolate

Instructions

1. Preheat the oven to 375 degrees C.
2. For preparing the crust. Mix crumbs, sugar, salt, and cinnamon in a bowl.
3. Add butter and egg white. Put crumb mixture in the up and bottom sides of a pie plate, and bake at 375 degrees C for around 9 minutes. Let it cool.
4. For preparing the filling, mix ingredients in a bowl.
5. Put milk in a saucepan over the medium heat. Gradually mix hot milk and egg mixture. Stir constantly.
6. Put milk mixture back to the pan. Cook until it is thick. Stir constantly.
7. Turn off the heat, then put chocolate in it. Stir smoothly.

8. Let it cool, then put filling in the crust. Put plastic wrap to cover it. Chill for 3 hours, then take off the plastic wrap.
9. Pour whipped topping, and sprinkle with cracker crumbs.
10. Serve and enjoy!

9.6 Horchata Cupcakes

Ingredients

For Cake:

- 2 sticks of butter
- 1 tsp. of vanilla extract
- 400 grams of granulated sugar

- 4 egg whites
- 360 grams of flour
- 225 grams of sour cream
- 1/2 tsp. of baking soda
- 2 tsp. of baking powder
- 1 tsp. of salt
- 1 1/4 cup of horchata
- 1 tsp. of ground cinnamon

For Buttercream:

- 115 grams of cream cheese
- 1 stick of butter
- 500 grams of powdered sugar
- 1 tsp. of ground cinnamon
- 1 tsp. of vanilla extract
- 2 tbsp. of horchata

Instructions

1. Preheat the oven to 350 degrees F.

2. Mix flour, baking powder, cinnamon, salt, and baking soda.
3. In a hand mixer, whisk the butter until it is creamy.
4. Mix sugar.
5. Put egg whites in it, and whip until the mixture is fluffy.
6. Put sour cream and vanilla in it.
7. Lower the heat, then mix dry ingredients.
8. Put horchata in it.
9. Fill the cupcake liners, and bake for around 15-18 minutes.
10. Let it cool before icing.
11. To prepare buttercream, whisk cream cheese, and butter.
12. Add powdered sugar.
13. Mix vanilla, cinnamon, and horchata in it. Mix until creamy and smooth.
14. Pour on the cupcakes and serve.

9.7 Traditional Flan Custard

Ingredients

- 6 eggs
- 1 1/2 cups of sugar
- 1 14-ounce can of condensed milk
- 1 tsp. of vanilla
- 1 can of evaporated milk
- 1 pinch of salt

Instructions

1. Preheat the oven to 325 degrees F.
2. To prepare caramel sauce, pour sugar into a pan over the medium heat. Stir constantly.
3. When it is brown and fully melted, it will become caramel.

4. Once the color reaches golden brown, transfer it to the pie plate.
5. To prepare the custard, whisk the eggs for one minute or until they are frothy.
6. Gradually put condensed milk in it, then the evaporated milk. Slowly mix the vanilla and sugar.
7. To bake the flan, put the custard mixture in the caramel pie plate.
8. Put the pie plate in a baking dish.
9. Bake the flan for around 45 minutes. Use a knife to check its status. If it is clean, then your flan is ready.
10. Remove the flan from the baking dish. Let it cool for overnight in the refrigerator for better taste.
11. Serve and enjoy!

9.8 Mexican Churros

Instructions

- 1 cup of water
- 4 cups of vegetable oil
- 1/2 cups of salted butter
- 1/4 tsp. of salt
- 1 tsp. of vanilla extract
- 1 cup flour
- 1 cup of sugar
- 3 eggs
- 1 tsp. of ground cinnamon

Instructions

1. Make the dough by mixing water, vanilla, salt, and butter in a saucepan. When the mixture starts to simmer, turn off the heat.
2. Add eggs one by one, mashing and stirring the dough until it is fully incorporated.
3. Put the mixture to a pastry bag.

4. Put the dough into the hot oil.
5. Cook it until it is puffy. Cook evenly from all sides. It will take 2-4 minutes.
6. Carefully take out churro from the oil, and use a paper towel to drain it.
7. When churros are cooled, put the cinnamon and sugar into a plastic bag.
8. Put churros in it and shake until they are coated.

9.9 Vegan Mexican Chocolate Cake

Ingredients

- 1 cup of sugar
- 1 1/2 cups of flour
- 1/4 cup of cocoa
- 1 1/2 tsp. cinnamon
- 1 tsp. baking soda
- 3/4 tsp. cayenne pepper
- 1 tbsp. white vinegar
- 1 tsp. vanilla
- 5 tbsp. vegetable oil
- 2 tbsp. of powdered sugar
- 1 cup of cold water

Instructions

1. Preheat the oven to 350 degrees F.
2. Grease a cake pan.
3. Take a bowl, and combine sugar, flour, cocoa, cinnamon, baking soda, and cayenne.
4. Mix vanilla, oil, vinegar, and water.
5. Put the mixture in the cake pan, then bake for almost 30 minutes.
6. Sprinkle powdered sugar, and serve.

9.10 Pan de Muerto

Ingredients

- 2 tbsp. of yeast
- 500 grams of flour
- 100 grams of sugar
- 80 grams of butter
- 1 tsp. salt
- 80 grams of unsalted margarine
- 2 oranges
- 4 eggs
- 60 ml. of warm water
- 1 egg
- 1 tsp. of orange essence
- Sugar, for decoration

Instructions

1. Place eggs, margarine, sugar, and salt in a mixer bowl.
2. Add the flour with the water. Then add yeast and mix to combine.
3. Add butter, orange zest, sugar, and orange essence. Mix to make a soft dough.
4. Knead the dough, and transfer it back to the bowl. Cover it with plastic wrap, and set aside for about 45 minutes.
5. Make pieces from the dough, and prepare greased baking sheets.
6. Place these pieces onto baking sheets. And press them slightly.
7. Preheat the oven to 350^0 C.
8. Mix a pinch of salt to the mixture of water and egg.
9. Brush it on the buns.
10. Transfer the buns/pieces to the oven. Bake until it is golden brown.
11. Let it cool at room temperature.

12. When the Pan de Muerto bread is cooled, brush it with butter and sprinkle with sugar.
13. Serve and enjoy!

9.11 Mexican Buñuelos

Ingredients

For Buñuelos:

- 1 1/2 tsp. baking powder
- 2 cups of flour
- 1/2 tsp. salt
- 4 tbsp. oil, for frying
- 3/4 cup of warm water

For Topping:

- 1 tbsp. of ground cinnamon
- 1/2 cup of granulated sugar

Instructions

1. Take a bowl, add salt, baking powder, and flour in it.
2. Add oil and warm water. Mix with your hands.
3. Make the dough and knead it for 8-10 minutes to make it smooth.
4. Cover it and set aside for 30 minutes.
5. Take a pan with frying oil in it and make a topping of cinnamon sugar.
6. Make balls from the dough, then shape them into circles.
7. Heat oil to 350 F, and fry each circle for 60 seconds, until it is golden brown from both sides.
8. Remove any excess oil, and sprinkle cinnamon sugar topping.
9. Serve and Enjoy!

9.12 Mexican Brownies

Ingredients

- 3/4 cup of dark chocolate chips
- 2 tsp. ground cinnamon
- 1 package of fudge brownie mix
- 1 tsp. of ancho chili pepper
- 1/2 cup of canola oil
- 2 eggs
- 1/4 cup of water

Instructions

1. Add brownie mix to spices.
2. Transfer this mixture to a glass jar.
3. Add chocolate chips, then cover it. You can store it in a cool and dry place for up to 3 months.
4. For brownies, preheat the oven to 350 degrees C.
5. Whisk together oil, eggs, and water.
6. Slowly add brownie mix and chocolate chips.
7. Spread it on a baking pan, then bake until or around 20-25 minutes.
8. Let it cool completely, and then serve.

Chapter 10: Most Famous Mexican Recipes

Cook and enjoy some of the most popular Mexican recipes, including tacos, burritos, and quesadillas.

10.1 Tacos Recipes

Marcela's Baja-style Fish Tacos

Ingredients

For Beer Batter:

- 1 cup Mexican beer
- 1 tsp. salt
- 1 cup flour
- 1/2 tsp. black peppe

For Cream Sauce:

- 2/3 cup sour cream
- 1/3 cup of mayonnaise
- 1 tsp. lemon zest
- 2 tbsp. water
- 2 tbsp. fresh lemon juice
- Salt, to taste
- Black pepper, to taste

For Fish Tacos:

- 1 cup flour
- Oil, to fry
- 1 tsp. salt
- Black pepper, to taste
- 2 pounds of skinned halibut
- 4 corn tortillas
- 2 cups of tomatillo salsa, for garnishing
- 2 cups f shredded cabbage
- Pickled jalapenos, optional

Instructions

For Beer Batter:

1. Put salt, pepper, and flour in a bowl.
2. Pour beer and whisk.
3. Set it aside for almost 15 minutes.

For Cream Sauce:

4. Mix crema and mayonnaise in a bowl.
5. Add lemon juice, lemon zest, and water.
6. Add pepper and salt.

For Fish:

7. Take a skillet, heat oil over the medium heat.
8. Take a plate, and combine salt and flour.
9. Cover the fish pieces flour and season with pepper and salt.
10. Dip fillets in beer batter, then cover both sides.
11. Fry until it is golden brown. Cook it thoroughly and put it on paper towels and drain.
12. Combine fish and tortillas.
13. Top with pickled jalapenos, shredded cabbage, cream, and tomatillo salsa.

Tacos Carne Asada

Ingredients

- 2 tbsp. fresh lime juice
- 2 tbsp. soy sauce
- 2 tbsp. canola oil
- 2 tsp. chili powder
- 3 cloves minced garlic
- 1 tsp. ground cumin
- 1 1/2 pounds of skirt steak
- 1 tsp. dried oregano
- 6 flour tortillas
- 1/2 cup of cilantro leaves

- 3/4 cup red onion, diced
- 1 lime

Instructions

1. Take a bowl, mix lime juice, soy sauce, oregano, canola oil, chili powder, garlic, and cumin.
2. Take a bowl, mix steak, and soy sauce mixture. Marinate for 1-4 hours.
3. Heat the remaining canola oil over the medium heat.
4. Put the steak in it and cook until brown.
5. Serve in tortillas and top with cilantro, onion, and lime.

Beef Barbacoa Tacos

Ingredients

- 4 minced cloves garlic
- 3 pounds of beef chuck roast
- 1 chopped white onion
- 1 can of green chiles
- 1/4 cup of lime juice
- 4 bay leaves
- 2 tbsp. of apple cider vinegar
- 1 tbsp. ground cumin
- 2 tsp. sea salt
- 1 tbsp. Mexican oregano, dried
- 1/4 tsp. ground cloves
- 1 tsp. black pepper
- 1/2 cup of beef stock

Instructions

1. In the slow cooker, mix all ingredients.
2. Cook it for 6-8 hours while keeping it covered until beef is cooked.
3. Shred beef into pieces.
4. Season with lemon juice, and cover it. Leave it for 10 minutes.

5. Take out the bay leaves, and serve.

Crispy Chicken Mini Tacos

Ingredients

- 1/2 cup white onion, chopped
- 1 cup tomato, chopped
- 1 jalapeno
- Salt, to taste
- Black pepper, to taste
- 1 tbsp. chopped cilantro leaves
- 1 chicken breast
- Vegetable oil, to fry
- 2 1/2 tbsp. olive oil
- 8 corn tortillas
- 3 tbsp. iceberg lettuce, shredded
- 1/4 cup sour cream
- 3 tbsp. feta or queso fresco cheese

Instructions

1. Mix onion, cilantro, tomato, and jalapeno in a bowl.
2. Add pepper and salt to taste. Then set it aside.
3. Preheat oven to the 350^0 F.
4. Apply olive oil on the chicken breast. Sprinkle with pepper and salt, to taste.
5. Roast the chicken for about 25 minutes.
6. Let it cool, then shred it.
7. Take a skillet and heat vegetable oil.
8. Put shredded chicken in the center of corn tortilla, then roll it.
9. Fry tacos until it is golden brown, then cut into half.
10. Top it with salsa and shredded lettuce.
11. Put queso fresco on it, and serve.

Pork Carnitas Tacos

Ingredients

For Canitas:

- 1 tbsp. lime juice
- 2 1/2 pounds of pork shoulder
- 2 tsp. sea salt
- 1 cup of broth, vegetable, chicken or beef
- 1 tsp. chili powder
- 2 tsp. ground cumin
- 1 tsp. garlic powder
- 1 tsp. onion powder
- 1 tsp. dried oregano
- 1/2 tsp. black pepper

Instructions

For Slow Cooker:

1. Make pieces of pork shoulder, and put them in a slow cooker.
2. Mix chili powder, salt, lime juice, ground cumin, garlic powder, dried oregano, onion powder, and black pepper.
3. Then coat the pork slices with seasonings.
4. Cook while keeping it covered for around 4 hours on medium heat.
5. When it is cooked, take out and shred.
6. Put chopped cilantro in it and serve in tacos.

For Instant Pot:

1. Make pieces of pork shoulder. Put them in an Instant Pot.
2. Mix salt, lime juice, ground cumin, garlic powder, chili powder, dried oregano, onion powder, broth, and black pepper.
3. Then coat the pork slices with seasonings.

4. Cook for around 40 minutes on high pressure.
5. Shred the pieces.
6. Add chopped cilantro, and serve in tacos.

Mushroom, Poblano, and Potato Tacos

Ingredients

- 3 medium potatoes, cut into pieces
- 4 poblano chile peppers
- Kosher salt, to taste
- 1 1/2 tbsp. fresh cilantro finely chopped
- 2 tbsp. olive oil
- 1 1/2 tbsp. fresh parsley, finely chopped
- 1 onion, sliced
- 2 tbsp. unsalted butter
- 12 ounces white mushrooms, sliced
- 1/2 cup of creme fraiche, Mexican crema, or sour cream
- 1 clove minced garlic
- 2 limes, juiced
- Corn tortillas, for serving
- Ground pepper, to taste

Instructions

1. Get a boiler or a gas burner, and roast poblanos for around 10 minutes.
2. Take it out in a bowl, then cover. Let it cool for around 10 minutes.
3. Cut them into strips.
4. Place potatoes in a nonstick skillet; cover them with cold water, and season with the salt.
5. Cook over the medium heat. Cook until they are tender, then drain.
6. Take a skillet and heat oil over the medium heat.
7. Put potatoes in it; cook until they are crisp and golden for 4 minutes.
8. Drain them on paper towels.

9. Sprinkle with salt and herbs.
10. Remove excess oil.
11. Take a skillet and heat butter over the medium heat.
12. Put the onion in it, and cook until it is golden.
13. Put mushrooms in it, and cook until they are golden.
14. Mix garlic and herbs; cook for 1 minute.
15. Put roasted poblanos, lime juice, crema, and some water; stir for 1-2 minutes.
16. Add pepper and salt.
17. Serve mushroom mixture and potatoes in tortillas with toppings.

Chipotle Chicken Meatball Tacos

Ingredients

- 1 egg
- 2 slices of white bread
- 1 finely chopped white onion
- 1/4 cup fresh cilantro, chopped
- 2 cloves minced garlic
- 3/4 pound of ground chicken
- Kosher salt, to taste
- Ground pepper, to taste
- 3 tbsp. olive oil
- 1 chipotle chile pepper, chopped
- 1 jalapeno pepper, chopped
- 1 can of diced tomatoes
- 1/4 tsp. ground cinnamon
- 1/4 tsp. dried thyme
- 3 bay leaves
- Taco shells, for serving

Instructions

1. Put egg and bread in a bowl.
2. Add water and then mash them.

3. Add garlic and onion, then put cilantro, chicken, pepper, and salt. Mix it well.
4. Brush a baking sheet with olive oil.
5. Make meatballs from the mixture and place on baking sheet, then pun in the refrigerator for around 15 minutes.
6. Preheat oven to 475^0 F.
7. Mix the remaining garlic and onion, jalapeno, chipotle, thyme, tomatoes, and cinnamon, and blend until smooth.
8. In the oven, heat olive oil over the medium heat.
9. Add tomato puree, and add bay leaves; cook until sauce thickens.
10. Add 1 1/2 cups of water.
11. Lower the heat and simmer; stir occasionally.
12. Add salt.
13. Bake meatballs until brown for 8 minutes.
14. Put it in the sauce and simmer.
15. Spoon sauce over meatballs, until they are thoroughly cooked
16. Remove bay leaves, and cut meatballs into halves.
17. Serve in tacos with toppings.

Quick Vegetarian Tacos

Ingredients

- 1 cup summer squash, chopped
- 1 Japanese eggplant, cut into pieces
- 1 bell pepper, red
- Olive oil, to drizzle
- 1 cup of cherry tomatoes
- 6 tortillas
- 1 diced avocados
- 1 cup of black beans, cooked
- Chopped cilantro
- Cotija cheese, crumbled, optional

- 1 serrano pepper, optional
- Sea salt, to taste
- Black pepper, to taste

For Sauce:

- 1/4 cup of pepitas
- 1/3 cup of tomatillo salsa
- 1/2 avocado
- 2 tbsp. of olive oil
- 2 tbsp. of spinach
- 1 tbsp. of lime juice
- Sea salt, to taste
- Black pepper, to taste

Instructions

1. Preheat oven to 400 degrees F.
2. Put chopped eggplant, red pepper, tomatoes, and squash in a baking sheet.
3. Add olive oil, pepper, and salt onto it, then roast until it is golden brown.
4. Blend tomatillo salsa, avocado, pepitas, spinach, olive oil, salt, lime juice, and pepper, and set aside.
5. Make tacos with roasted vegetables, black beans, diced avocado, serrano, cilantro, and cotija.
6. Serve with more sauce.

Tex-Mex Taco Pizza

Ingredients

- 1 1 1/2 pounds of pizzeria dough
- 1 cup of jarred salsa
- 1 cup of Cheddar cheese, shredded
- 1 onion, chopped
- 1 tbsp. of olive oil
- 2 tsp. of ground cumin
- 1 tsp. of smoked paprika

- 1 tsp. of garlic powder
- 1 pound of beef sirloin
- 1/4 cup of sour cream
- 1/2 cup pickled jalapeno
- 1 tbsp. of lime juice
- 1 heart thinly sliced romaine lettuce
- 1 tbsp. of milk
- 2 small chopped plum tomatoes

Instruction

1. Preheat the oven to 475^0 F.
2. Pour salsa all over the dough. Put cheddar on it and bake.
3. Take a skillet and heat oil.
4. Add cumin, onion, smoked paprika, and garlic powder, then cook for 3 minutes.
5. Mix beef and salt, and cook for 3 more minutes until brown.
6. Add beef on cheese.
7. Add jalapenos. Then bake for almost 20 minutes.
8. Mix sour cream with milk and lime juice.
9. Put tomatoes and lettuce on top of the pizza.
10. Pour sour cream mixture, and serve.

10.2 Burritos Recipes

Beef and Bean Burritos

Ingredients

- 2 tbsp. taco seasoning
- 1 pound ground beef
- 6 tortillas, flour
- 1 cup Mexican cheese, shredded
- 16 ounces refried bean

Instructions

1. Put beef in a skillet over the high heat; add taco seasoning in it.
2. Cook until it is brown, then drain and set aside.
3. Assemble burritos by putting flour tortilla in the microwave for almost 20 seconds.
4. Put a layer of refried beans, cheese, and then cooked beef on it.
5. Fold the sides and bottom of the tortilla.
6. Wrap it in a parchment paper; if you like to store in the refrigerator for up to 30 days.
7. To serve and eat, wrap it in the paper towel; microwave for around 2-3 minutes, set it aside for almost one minute.
8. Enjoy!

Ultimate Vegan Burrito

Ingredients

- 2 mushroom caps
- 2 cups of Spanish Rice, cooked
- 1/2 red onion
- 2 cans of black beans
- 1 bell pepper, orange
- 2 tbsp. olive oil
- 1 tsp. garlic powder
- 2 tsp. cumin
- 1 tsp. onion powder
- 1 tsp. kosher salt
- 1 tsp. smoked paprika
- 2 tbsp. lime juice
- 4 large tortillas
- 1 avocado

Instructions

1. Remove stems from mushroom caps; cut into slices.

2. Slice bell pepper and red onion.
3. Take a skillet, and heat oil over the medium heat.
4. Cook veggies for almost 6-7 minutes.
5. Put black beans, garlic powder, onion powder, cumin, paprika, lime juice, kosher salt, and some water. Cook until liquid evaporates.
6. Add kosher salt to the mashed avocado.
7. To assemble tortilla, put 1/2 cup of rice on it. Top with the bean mixture, avocado, and vegetable.
8. Fold in all sides of burritos.
9. Cut them, and serve.

Burrito Egg Rolls

Ingredients

- 1/2 cup of black beans
- 1/2 pounds of ground beef
- 1 cup cheddar cheese
- 1/4 cup green pepper
- 1/2 cup of frozen corn
- 1 tsp. taco seasoning
- 14 egg roll wrappers
- 1 tsp. olive oil
- 1 tomato, diced
- Oil, to fry
- Salt, to taste
- Pepper, to taste
- Guacamole, to serve

Instructions

1. Take a skillet, and heat oil over the medium heat.
2. Put taco seasoning and beef in it—season with pepper and salt.
3. Drain fat from beef and put it back to skillet.
4. Put back beans and corn, and cook for 2 minutes.
5. Turn off the heat and take it out in a bowl.

6. Add shredded cheddar, green pepper, and tomato in it.
7. Put the mixture and the egg roll wrapper in the center. Roll it, and continue this process with all burrito mixture and egg roll wrappers.
8. Take a skillet, and heat oil over the medium heat.
9. Fry each side of egg roll until it is golden brown.
10. Turn off the heat; drain the fat.
11. Repeat the process with other egg rolls.
12. Serve immediately with the guacamole.

Cabbage Burritos

Instructions

- 1 tbsp. olive oil
- 8 cabbage leaves
- 1/2 chopped onion
- 2 cloves minced garlic
- 1 pound ground beef
- 1 tbsp. of taco seasoning mix
- Black pepper, to taste
- Kosher salt to taste
- 1 can of black beans
- 1/2 cup shredded cheddar
- 1 cup corn, frozen or canned
- 1 1/2 cup of cherry tomatoes, chopped
- 1 cup of Monterey Jack, shredded

Instructions

1. Preheat the oven to the 350°C.
2. In boiling water, dip cabbage leaves for 30 seconds. Pat them dry.
3. Take a skillet, and heat oil over the medium heat.
4. Put the onion in it and cook for 5 minutes.
5. Add garlic and ground beef. Cook for about 5 minutes.
6. Add taco seasoning mix, pepper, and salt.
7. Add cherry tomatoes, black beans, and corn.

8. Place cabbage leaves on a plate, and put beef mixture with cheese.
9. Fold cabbage leaves, then roll them.
10. Bake them until for around 10 minutes.

Cheesy Baked Burritos

Instructions

- 1 chopped onion
- 1 tbsp. olive oil
- 2 minced garlic cloves
- 1 cup enchilada sauce
- Kosher salt to taste
- 2 cup of rotisserie chicken
- 1 lime, juiced
- Black pepper,
- to taste
- 1 can of black beans
- 1 cup cheddar cheese
- 2 cup of white rice, cooked
- 1 cup cheese, Monterey Jack
- Sour cream, optional
- Chopped cilantro, optional
- 6 flour tortillas
- Hot sauce, optional

Instructions

1. Preheat the oven to 350^0 F.
2. Take a skillet, and heat oil over the medium heat.
3. Put onion and cook until soft.
4. Add garlic for around 30 seconds.
5. Put enchilada sauce and chicken in it.
6. Add lime juice; season with pepper and salt.
7. Put a tortilla on a board. Add beans and rice on top of it.

8. Put in chicken mixture, and top with both kinds of cheese.
9. Roll burrito and put in a dish.
10. Put enchilada sauce on burritos; sprinkle extra cheeses.
11. Cook for around 15 minutes.
12. Add cilantro; serve with hot sauce and sour cream.

Low-Carb Breakfast Burritos

Instructions

- 1 tbsp. of skim milk
- Kosher salt to taste
- 2 eggs
- 1 tbsp. of chopped chives
- Black pepper, to taste
- 1 tbsp. of butter
- 1/2 cup of black beans
- 4 slices bacon, cooked
- 1 avocado, sliced
- Salsa, to serve
- 1/2 cup of shredded cheddar

Instructions

1. Take a bowl, and mix eggs, chives, and milk; season with pepper and salt.
2. Take a skillet, and melt butter in it.
3. Add the egg mixture in it. Cook each side for almost 2 minutes.
4. Place it on a plate; top with black beans, bacon, avocado, salsa, and cheddar.
5. Make a burrito, then serve.

Burrito Avocados

Instructions

- 1/4 finely chopped onion
- 1 tbsp. of olive oil

- 1/2 pounds of ground beef
- 1/2 tsp. of ground cumin
- 1/2 tsp. of chili powder
- 1/2 tsp. of garlic powder
- Black pepper, to taste
- Kosher salt, to taste
- 1/2 cup of frozen corn
- Sliced Cheddar
- 2 avocados
- Monterey Jack, sliced
- 1/4 cup of cherry tomatoes
- 2 tsp. fresh cilantro, for garnishing
- Sour cream, for garnishing

Instructions

1. Take a skillet, and heat oil over the medium heat.
2. Put the onion in it and cook for 5 minutes.
3. Put ground beef and cook for around 6 minutes.
4. Add spices, and season with pepper and salt.
5. Add frozen corn, and cook.
6. Cut slices of avocado.
7. Put avocado on the serving plate.
8. Put cheese slices between cuts, and top with beef mixture.
9. Add sour cream and cilantro.
10. Serve.

Frito Pie Burritos

Ingredients

For Burritos:

- 1 cup of chili con carne
- 4 flour tortillas
- 1 cup of Fritos
- 3/4 cup of refried beans
- 1/2 cup of corn kernels

- 1 cup of cheddar cheese

For Toppings:

- 1/4 cup of minced red onions
- ½ cup of fresh diced tomatoes
- ¼ cup of chopped cilantro
- ½ cup of shredded lettuce
- Lime wedges
- 1 sliced jalapeno
- 1/4 cup of sour cream

Instructions

1. Fill tortillas with corn, chili, Fritos, cheese, and refried beans.
2. Heat a skillet over the medium heat; grease with pan spray.
3. Cook each side of burritos for about 3 minutes until it is golden brown.
4. Serve with toppings.

Steak Burrito

Ingredients

- 2 tsp. of ground cumin
- 1/2 pound of skirt steak
- 2 minced cloves garlic
- 4 tbsp. olive oil
- 2 limes, juiced
- 1 can of black beans
- kosher salt, to taste
- 3 tomatoes, finely diced
- Black pepper, to taste
- 1/3 cup of red onion, minced
- 1 diced avocado
- 5 tbsp. of chopped cilantro
- 1 cup of rice, cooked

- 1 1/2 cups of romaine lettuce, thinly sliced
- Sour cream
- 4 tortillas
- Cheddar cheese, shredded

Instructions

1. Take a bowl, and add steak with garlic clove, cumin, lime juice, and olive oil.
2. Take a skillet, and heat oil over the medium heat.
3. Put remaining garlic and cook for 1 minute.
4. Put black beans in it and cook for 4-5 minutes.
5. Add pepper and salt and mix lime juice.
6. Take a bowl, and stir tomatoes, cilantro, red onion, lime juice, and olive oil, avocado, pepper, and salt.
7. Heat the grill pan over the high heat.
8. Add steak, pepper, and salt; cook for 2-3 minutes.
9. In a bowl, mix rice, cilantro, pepper, and salt.
10. Brush a skillet with olive oil.
11. Put tortillas in it, and crisp each side for 30 seconds.
12. On each tortilla, put rice, beans, pico de gallo, avocado, steak slices, lettuce, cheese, and sour cream.
13. Roll the tortilla. Put burritos back to the skillet, and cook for 30 seconds.
14. Cut in half and serve.

Chicken and Avocado Burritos

Instructions

- 1 package of taco seasoning
- 1 pound chicken
- 1 tbsp. olive oil
- 2 avocados, diced
- 4 flour tortillas
- 1/4 cup of cilantro leaves, chopped
- 1 cup mozzarella cheese, shredded
- 1/4 cup of Ranch dressing

- 1/4 cup of sour cream

Instructions

1. Take a skillet and heat oil over the medium heat.
2. Add taco seasoning to chicken.
3. Cook chicken in the skillet until golden for around 3-4 minutes, then set it aside.
4. Warm the tortillas.
5. Take a tortilla and place chicken, cheese, avocado, sour cream, cilantro, and Ranch. Fold it, and continue this process with all tortillas.
6. Take a pan, and heat it over the medium heat.
7. Put burritos in it; cook each side for around 3 to 4 minutes until it is golden brown.
8. Serve immediately.

10.3 Quesadillas Recipes

BBQ Chicken Quesadillas

Izgredients

- 3 cups of cooked chicken breast
- 10 ounces of rice, cooked
- 1 can of kidney or red beans
- 3 cups Cheddar cheese, shredded
- 1 cup of barbecue sauce
- 6 tortillas

Instructions

1. Take a pan and heat beans and chicken with the BBQ sauce.
2. Add cooked rice, the bean and chicken mixture.
3. Put more sauce if you like.
4. To assemble the quesadillas, sprinkle cheddar cheese.
5. Then add cheese on chicken mixture. Use additional cheese if you like.

6. On each quesadilla, place another tortilla, and set aside.
7. Take a pan and toast quesadillas over the medium heat, then cook them until they are brown.
8. Serve and Enjoy!

Black Bean, Corn, and Wild-rice Quesadillas

Ingredients

- 1 cup of Cheddar cheese, shredded
- 10 ounces of rice, cooked
- 1/2 cup of black beans
- 2 chopped green onions
- 1/2 cup of mild salsa
- 1/2 cup of sweet corn, frozen
- 4 flour tortillas

Instructions

1. Add rice, beans, shredded cheese, green onions, and corn in a bowl.
2. Put 1/4 of this mixture on a tortilla.
3. Add mild salsa on the top. Fold the tortilla.
4. Heat a pan over the medium heat.
5. Put a quesadilla in the pan, and cook until it is golden brown.
6. Cook all the remaining quesadillas.
7. Let them cool, and then cut them in half.
8. Serve with salsa.

Mashed Potato Quesadilla

Ingredients

- 6 slices of bacon, cooked and crumbled
- 2 cups of mashed potatoes
- ¼ cup of green onions, sliced
- 2 cups of Cheddar cheese, shredded
- 1/4 cup of sour cream
- 8 flour tortillas

- 1 cup of salsa
- 2 tbsp. of softened butter

Instructions

1. Mix mashed potatoes, green onions, and bacon.
2. Put this mixture on the tortillas.
3. Add shredded cheese on the top and put remaining tortillas on the top.
4. Put butter on each side of quesadillas.
5. Heat a skillet over the medium heat.
6. Put quesadilla in the pan; cook each side until it is crispy and golden brown.
7. Repeat this process with all quesadillas, then serve with sour cream and salsa.

Shrimp Quesadillas

Ingredients

- 1 sliced onion
- 2 tbsp. of vegetable oil
- 1 bell pepper, red
- 1 tsp. salt
- 1 bell pepper, green
- 1 tsp. ground cumin
- 1 pound shrimp, uncooked
- 1 tsp. chili powder
- 3 cups Mexican cheese, shredded
- 1 jalapeno pepper, minced
- 1 tsp. of vegetable oil
- 1 lime, juiced
- 6 flour tortillas

Instructions

1. Heat oil in a pan over the medium heat.
2. Add onion, green, and red bell pepper; stir frequently. Cook for 6-8 minutes.

3. Add cumin, salt, and chili powder.
4. Add shrimp and cook for 3-5 minutes.
5. Turn off the heat.
6. Add lime juice and jalapeno pepper in shrimp mixture.
7. Heat a pan over the medium heat; brush it with vegetable oil.
8. Put a tortilla in it. Place shrimp filling and cheese blend on it, and then fold the tortilla.
9. Cook each side for around 5 minutes.
10. Repeat the same process with all tortillas.
11. Serve and enjoy!

Peanut Butter Quesadillas

Ingredients

- 2 tbsp. grape jelly
- 1 flour tortilla
- 1 tsp. butter
- 2 tbsp. peanut butter

Instructions

1. Melt butter in a pan over the medium heat.
2. Put peanut butter on tortilla.
3. Fold it in half.
4. Put it in the pan, and heat each side for two minutes, until it is brown.
5. Cut into wedges, then dip it in jelly and serve.

Conclusion

Mexican cuisine has some amazingly loved and popular dishes in the world. It varies by area due to geography, local climate, and ethnic differences. One common thing about Mexican food is its spiciness. Mexican food can easily be recognized as spicy and hot. The use of chiles is the big reason behind it. Its use is more sophisticated in Mexico than in any other place. Many people from other cultures use chiles the way Mexicans use to add texture and flavor in their food. That is the reason, different varieties of chiles are used as each one serves a different purpose. It is used in making salsa. Many Mexican recipes have the use of salsa to add particular flavor.

Vegetables play a crucial part in Mexican food. The use of tomatoes, potatoes, corn, mushrooms, etc. has always been part of traditional Mexican cuisine. The addition of meat makes the Mexican food rich in protein. All ingredients have the unique feature that they brought to the colorful cuisine of Mexican food. So, it is a perfect and healthy combination of proteins and carbs.

Many countries have made slight changes in the Mexican recipes and added a little bit of flavor to their own cultures. You can see it in the famous Mexican food version in the United States named 'Ted-Mex'. But, if you want to try adventure with your taste buds, try at least once the authentic Mexican food. One of the differences between Mexican food and Ted-Mex is the type of cheese used in recipes. In Ted-Mex, yellow cheese is used, while in authentic Mexican recipes, white cheese is used. The other notable differences are in the use of spices, and the type of tortillas. Both versions of the Mexican food offer delicious recipes. It is up to the Mexican food-lovers, whether they want a little bit change, or want to stick to the authentic taste of Mexican food.

The traditional Mexican cooking style is very humble and earthy. So, if you like to cook at home and try delicious Mexican recipes, but feel unsure of your cooking skills, use this 'Mexican Food' cookbook for cooking and enjoying your favorite recipes. Find your favorite recipes for each time of the day in this cookbook. Create a Mexican-style treat at home, from Steak Burrito to Mexican Churros, and some famous Mexican rice, tacos, soups, and fajitas. It is just difficult not to fell in love with authentic as well as modern-day Mexican food. It is not short on flavors at all.

All these Mexican dishes are worth a try. Some dishes are quick to make, but some will take time. When you have the final dish on your table, you will be satisfied with all the effort you put in. Do not hesitate to customize a little bit as per your preferences and health goals.

Made in the USA
Middletown, DE
20 October 2020

22430950R00076